Lessons
with
Laughter

George Woolard

LTP
LANGUAGE

Language Teaching Publications
114a Church Road, Hove, BN3 2EB, England

ISBN 1 899396 35 7
© LTP 1996, 1997, 1998, 1999

The Author
George Woolard is an experienced ELT teacher who has worked in Greece and Malaysia. He now teaches a wide range of English courses at Stevenson College, Edinburgh.

Acknowledgements
Cover design by Anna Macleod
Simon Girling Associates, Martin Cater, and Peter Wilks for the illustrations
Punch Publications and Private Eye for permission to use the cartoons in Lessons 30-38
Printed in England by Commercial Colour Press Plc, London E7.

Introduction

Lessons with humour

Most teaching materials are not humorous. If there is humour in the classroom, it comes from the teacher and the students. **Lessons with Laughter** is designed to bring humour into your lessons. When students find something humorous, their learning becomes more enjoyable and their motivation increases. The lessons in the four sections of this book bring humour and English together.

Let them discover the humour

You cannot teach humour. If you have to explain it, it is no longer funny. The secret of the lessons in this book is to allow your students to discover the humour for themselves. Most often humour grows out of a language situation with more than one meaning – usually there is a well-known literal meaning plus a metaphorical meaning. Your role as teacher is not to lead your students by the hand through the wonderful world of British humour. Your role is to set up lessons where students can discover meaning for themselves: you will need to give them time to do this. You may explain the odd word. You will definitely encourage the use of dictionaries. And you will monitor the outcome of the problem-solving activities. If some in the class cannot see the joke, it is better to let the others in the class explain it – even if they have to do so in their own language. Resist the temptation to be the class comedian.

This is serious learning

When you find something amusing, you are more liable to remember it. When students discover new meanings for themselves, they are more likely to remember them because they laughed. This means that language items contained in humorous texts are more likely to be retained than if you had simply taught them in a conventional way. Students will want to retell the jokes and stories to other students, thereby reinforcing their learning.

A Lexical Approach

More and more teachers are seeing the advantages of taking a lexical approach to language. The jokes and stories in this book are full of useful word partnerships, fixed expressions, and sentence heads.

Four sections

The four sections of lessons exploit the four common types of humorous text:

1   Jokes – understanding double meaning
2   Cartoons – predicting and understanding captions
3   Misprints – finding and understanding them
4   Reading for Fun – graded funny stories with an amusing last line

The lessons and the sections are not designed to be used in any particular order. This book is a resource from which you can draw whatever you find suitable. The lessons in sections 1 – 3 are 'fillers' which you can use whenever you feel the need for something lighter. The Reading for Fun Section contains one page stories, many of which will take a whole lesson to read and exploit. The Misprints and Reading sections make motivating homework.

As the author of this material, I have heard much laughter in my classes. I hope your classes will have as much fun as mine have had.

George Woolard
Edinburgh 1996

Contents

Section One: Jokes

Section Two: Cartoons

Section Three: Misprints

Section Four: Reading for Fun

Elementary

Intermediate

Advanced

Answer Key

Section One

Jokes

The worksheets in this section consist mainly of two-line jokes in English. In some of them the first and second lines of these jokes have been separated on the worksheets in order to create a simple matching exercise.

Procedure

Give students the worksheet and ask them to complete it. With weaker classes it is useful to do one example with them. Alternatively, cut the worksheet in two and give out the upper part and ask them to read and suggest possible answers. Then give them the lower part and ask them to complete the matching exercise.

The amount of pre-teaching of vocabulary necessary during the setting up of the activity will depend on the class. Keep to the literal meaning of words and phrases. Let the students infer any non-literal meaning.

Remember the guiding principle – it is the students who tell each other jokes. Resist the temptation as teacher to become the class comedian.

If necessary, work through an example to clarify the processing which leads the student to an understanding of non-literal meaning. For example, one way of getting students to understand the idiom 'to pull somebody's leg' is simply to tell them that it means ' to play a joke or trick on somebody.' An alternative approach is to provide them with a context in which they can work this out for themselves. The first lesson **Idioms** is designed to do this. Note that the students are faced with an initial problem, a matching exercise which can be completed from an understanding of literal meaning only. On this basis the student will match:

Why can't you play jokes on snakes?   with   **Because you can't pull their legs.**

The fact that this is a joke and is by definition intended to be humorous, presents the students with a second problem and, therefore, motivates a further search for meaning. The students can work out that there must be a relationship between 'to play a joke on somebody' and 'to pull somebody's leg'. If the students then infer that they mean the same, then the problem is solved and the students have discovered the joke for themselves *and* learned a new idiom in the process. Once the student has reached this stage the teacher can confirm the students' inferencing and add further comments on the language in focus.

Finally, students will want to retell the jokes they find funny to their friends and this provides a natural form of language practice and reinforcement.

1 Idioms

Can you complete these jokes? Try first without looking at the answers. Each answer depends on a common English idiom. Do you understand each one?

1   Why can't you play jokes on snakes?

> ....

2   When is an actor happy to become a thief?

> ....

3   My mother made a terrible mistake today. She gave my father soapflakes instead of cornflakes for breakfast.
> Was he angry?

> ....

"More flakes, dear?"

4   Two flies flew onto a coffee cup and argued about who arrived first and who should get to drink the cold coffee. Which one got angry and left?

> ....

5   Why is it impossible to play tennis quietly?

> ....

6   How could you help a starving cannibal?

> ....

7   When does a patient find an operation funny?

> ....

8   Why did the tired man put his bed in the fireplace?

> ....

9   When are mosquitoes annoying?

> ....

A   When he steals the show.

B   He wanted to sleep like a log.

C   Only foaming at the mouth.

D   Give him a hand.

E   Because you can never pull their legs.

F   The one that flew off the handle.

G   When it leaves him in stitches.

H   When they get under your skin.

I   Because you can't play it without raising a racket.

2 Phrasal Verbs

Complete each joke with a verb. Try to do it without looking at the list of verbs at the bottom of the page. Each verb makes up a phrasal verb. Underline them all.

1   Doctor, Doctor, I can't sleep at night.
>   Sleep on the edge of the bed and you'll soon . . . . . . off.

2   Why are ghosts bad at telling lies?
>   Because you can always . . . . . . through them.

3   Why do birds in a nest always agree?
>   Because they don't want to . . . . . . out.

4   When is a deep-sea diver disappointed with his colleagues?
>   When they . . . . . . him down.

5   What training do you need to become a rubbish collector?
>   None, you . . . . . . it up as you go along.

6   Waiter, I asked you to bring my order quickly but why is the food on my plate all squashed?
>   Well sir, when you ordered your food, you did tell me to
. . . . . . on it.

7   Why do taxi-drivers always go bankrupt?
>   Because they . . . . . . their customers away.

8   Wife: Did you . . . . . . the cat out, dear?
Sarcastic Husband: No. Was it on fire?

9   When are the traffic police strong?
>   When they . . . . . . up cars with one hand.

"Did you put the cat out, dear?"

see	put	drop
pick	hold	let
drive	fall	step

3 Word Partnerships

A word partnership – or collocation – is two or more words which go together in a special
way – *a golden opportunity*. Complete the following jokes with word partnerships.

1   What does an angry kangaroo do?

      > It gets . . . . mad.

2   Doctor, when I go to bed I wake up every thirty minutes.

      > Are you a . . . . sleeper?

      No, I sleep in the dark.

3   You're late for school again. What's your excuse?

      > I sprained my ankle and I couldn't walk properly, sir.

      That's a . . . . excuse.

"Ever seen an angry kangaroo?"

4   Why did the burglar take a shower?

      > He wanted to make a . . . . getaway.

5   I've invented a new pill. Half of the pill is aspirin and the other half is glue.

      > But who is it for?

      People with . . . . headaches.

6   What did the hooligan say after breaking all the school windows?

      > I've had a . . . . time.

7   Did you hear about the undertaker who buried somebody in the wrong cemetery?

      > He lost his job for making such a . . . . mistake.

8   Why do you put lumps of sugar under your pillow?

      > So that I will have . . . . dreams.

9   What do you call a millionaire who never washes?

      > . . . . rich.

clean	hopping	filthy
splitting	grave	sweet
light	lame	smashing

4 Puns

A pun is a play upon words – usually one word with two meanings. For example, a *mouse* is both an animal and something you use with a computer. Complete these jokes with puns.

1   Have you noticed any .... in me?
    > No! Why?
    I've just swallowed some coins accidentally.

2   Some girls think I'm handsome and some girls think
    I'm horrible. What do you think, Mary?
    > A bit of both, ...

3   You have to be rich to play golf.
    > Then why are there so many ....
    players?

4   I think we've just had a puncture.
    > How did it happen?
    There was a .... in the road.

"What's caused that puncture?"

5   Well son, how was your first day at the new school?
    > Great! The teacher is going to give me a gift.
    How do you know that?
    > Well, when I arrived, she pointed to a chair in the corner and said, "Sit over
    there for the ....

6   Why did the two astronauts decide to leave the restaurant on the moon and return
    to one on Earth?
    > They said it had no ....

7   I'm going to have to put you in a prison cell for the night.
    > What's the .... , Officer?
    Nothing. It's all part of the service!

8   Why did you park your car on the yellow lines?
    > Because the sign says '........   FOR PARKING'.

9   What do you call a happy tin in the USA?
    > A .... !

present	fork	fine
pretty ugly	atmosphere	merry can
change	charge	poor

5 Homophones

Homophones are two words which have the same sound but different meanings. Complete the following jokes. The humour depends on homophones in each one.

1   Waiter, what do you call this?
    > It's . . . . soup, sir.
    I don't care what it's . . . . What is it now?

2   Have you ever hunted . . . . ?
    > No, I always hunt with my clothes on.

3   Why are black clouds like somebody riding a horse?
    > Because they both hold the . . . .

"Have you ever hunted . . . . ?"

4   A teacher saw two boys fighting in the playground.
    > Stop! You know the school rules – No fighting . . . .
    But, sir, we weren't fighting . . . . We were fighting quietly.

5   What is the effect of seven days dieting?
    > They make one . . . .

6   Did you hear about the novelist who lived on the ninth floor of a block of flats?
    > He dropped six . . . . into a wastepaper basket and lived.

7   How can I get rid of my headache?
    > Hit your head against a window and the . . . . will disappear.

8   Fortune Teller: Would you like your palm . . . . , sir?
    Man: No thanks, I like the colour it is now.

9   What did the small shy stone say?
    > I wish I was a little . . . .

read / red	stories / storeys	rains / reins
bean / been	bolder / boulder	pane / pain
bare / bear	allowed / aloud	week / weak

6 Unusual Expressions

Some words with quite common meanings can be used in word partnerships with meanings which are difficult to guess. Complete the following more unusual expressions.

1   What happened to the thief who stole a kilometre of elastic?
    > He was put in prison for a long . . . .

2   When does a boat show its affection?
    > When it . . . . the shore.

3   Did you hear about the cat that came first
    in the milk-drinking competition?
    > It won by six . . . .

"Lapping it up!"

4   What do you do if you split your sides laughing?
    > Run until you get a . . . .

5   Did you hear about the optician who fell into his lens-grinding machine?
    > He made a . . . . of himself.

6   What does a king do after he burps?
    > He issues a royal . . . .

7   How can broken bones be productive?
    > When they begin to . . . . together.

8   Why did the ant rush across the top of a cereal packet?
    > Because it said ' . . . . along the dotted line' on the packet.

9   Ten pedigree dogs have escaped from their kennels and the police have been unable to recapture them. They say they have no . . . . and are appealing to the public for help.

spectacle	laps	tear
knit	stretch	leads
pardon	hugs	stitch

7 Missing Words

All the missing words from these jokes make a natural expression.

1 A millionaire who doesn't wash is someone who is . . . . rich.

2 While repairing his television Mr Smith touched a live electric wire. When he recovered, he described it as a . . . . experience.

3 A fireman always gets a . . . . reception wherever he goes.

"He's a bit of a live wire!"

4 It is a complete waste of time telling bald men . . . . stories.

5 The man who fell into a large tank of glue came to a . . . . end.

6 A politician had such a bad reputation for being dishonest that he decided to grow a beard so nobody could call him a . . . . liar.

7 She is certainly a . . . . beauty! She slapped me twice!

8 My husband is a man of . . . . gifts. He hasn't given me a present for years.

9 "John, I know that we have a large crack in the living-room wall, but will you stop telling people that you come from a . . . . home."

shocking	striking	rare
warm	broken	bare-faced
sticky	hair-raising	stinking

8 Moving Stress

All these jokes depend on how you say something – a change in the stress of one or two words – *along* the road and *a long* road.

1   Why didn't the skeleton go to the party?
> It had . . . . to go with.

2   Have you ever seen a . . . . ?
> No. How does it hold the rod?

3   Why are fishmongers so mean?
> Because their job makes them . . . .

4   What did Mrs Christmas say to Father Christmas when a thunderstorm started?
> Come and look at the . . . .

5   Instructor: Tomorrow you can fly . . . .
Trainee pilot: How low?

6   A policeman was overtaking a car when he was surprised to see an old lady knitting while driving. He wound down his window and shouted to her, " . . . ."
> No, a pair of socks! she replied.

7   First woman: Men are all . . . . !
Second woman: Yes, men are all . . . . !

8   Why are travel guides like handcuffs?
> Because they are made for . . . .

9   My uncle is an . . . .
> Is he?
Yes. He used to carry suitcases at the Sheraton Hotel.

"He's got my uncle's old job."

A   pull over / pullover

B   ex-porter / exporter

C   two wrists / tourists

D   no body / nobody

E   rain dear / reindeer

F   cat fish / catfish

G   alike / I like

H   so low / solo

I   sell fish / selfish

9 Misunderstandings

All the jokes on this page depend on a misunderstanding which is caused by stressing or pronouncing words in different ways.

1 Can you telephone from an aeroplane?

> . . . .

2 Teacher: John, give me a sentence with 'centimetre' in it.
John: . . . .

3 What did the electrician's wife ask him when he arrived home late?

> . . . .

4 Teacher: Mary, give me a sentence with 'gruesome' in it.
Mary: . . . .

5 An Eskimo who had just finished building a new igloo called his wife and asked her what she thought of the new house.
"Oh," she said, "It's . . . . house."

6 Teacher: George, give me a sentence with 'unaware' in it.
George: . . . .

7 Jim: I've just had my appendix out.
John: . . . .
Jim: No thanks, I don't smoke.

8 Teacher: Sarah, give me a sentence with 'fascinate' in it.
Sarah: . . . .

9 Where does your mother come from?

> . . . .
Never mind, I'll ask her myself.

A My underwear is the first thing I put on in the morning.

B an ice

C I had ten buttons on my shirt but I lost two, so now I can only fasten eight.

D Wire you insulate?

E When my aunt was arriving at the station I was sent to meet her.

F Sure, anybody can tell a phone from an aeroplane.

G Alaska.

H My dad grew some potatoes in the garden.

I Will you have a scar?

10   Books and their Authors

This is a common type of joke in English where the name of the author is related in meaning to the title of the book.

1   Late for School   by   . . . .

2   The Burglar   by   . . . .

3   A Present for a Lady   by   . . . .

4   Sleepless Nights   by   . . . .

5   Solo Attempt on Mt. Everest by   . . . .

6   Falling From A Window   by   . . . .

7   Solitude   by   . . . .

8   Top of the Class   by   . . . .

9   George Goes on Trial   by   . . . .

10 My Beautiful Flower   by   . . . .

A   Eliza Wake

B   I. Malone

C   C. Myra Port

D   Robin Holmes

E   Ivor Rose

F   Watts E. Dunn

G   Miss D. Buss

H   Willie Maykit

I   Sheila Dorrit

J   Eileen Dowt

11   Present Perfect Jokes

All the following jokes contain examples of the Present Perfect. When you have agreed on the missing line, go back and underline all uses of that tense.

1   Grocer, are these eggs fresh?
    > . . . .

2   How do we know that carrots are good for the eyes?
    > . . . .

3   My doctor says I can't play tennis.
    > . . . .

4   Dentist: Calm down. I haven't touched your tooth yet.
    Patient: . . . .

5   I've been singing since I was three.
    > . . . .

6   I could marry anyone I please.
    > Then why are you still single?
    . . . .

7   I've received hundreds of replies to my advertisement for a husband and they all
    say the same thing.
    > What's that?
    . . . .

8   Dentist: That's the biggest cavity I've ever seen, the biggest cavity I've ever seen.
    Patient: Why are you repeating yourself?
    Dentist: . . . .

9   This crossword is the most difficult one I've ever done. I've been trying to think of
    one word for two weeks.
    > . . . .

A   I haven't pleased anyone yet.
B   How about 'fortnight'?
C   Well, the chickens haven't missed them yet.
D   No wonder you've lost your voice.
E   Take mine!
F   I'm not – it was an echo.
G   Have you ever seen a rabbit wearing glasses?
H   I know, but you're standing on my foot.
I   So he has played with you as well.

12   Conditional Jokes

All the following jokes contain examples of the Conditional. When you have agreed on the answers, go back and underline all the verbs in the conditional clause.

1   If we get engaged to be married, will you give me a ring?
> . . . .

2   If you found some money, would you keep it?
> No. I would . . . .

3   Fish 1: How did we end up in this fish shop?
Fish 2: Well, ...

4   If the baby wakes up during the night, who gets up?
> . . . .

5   If you dial 2136543456783452678923456432234234567833123422247893456, what will you get?
> . . . .

6   Darling, if the boat sank, who would you save first, me or the children?
> . . . .

7   If you fall out of that tree and break your legs, ...

8   What would you do if you were in my shoes?
> . . . .

9   Two birds were sitting on a branch of a tree watching a jet plane pass high overhead.
"Look at the speed of that bird," said the youngest bird.
" . . . . " replied the older bird.

A   Polish them.
B   If your tail was on fire, you would fly just as fast,
C   A blister on your finger.
D   don't come running to me.
E   Sure. What's your phone number?
F   if we hadn't opened our mouths, we wouldn't have been caught.
G   spend it.
H   Me.
I   The whole neighbourhood.

13 Comparative Jokes

All the following jokes contain examples of comparatives. When you have agreed on the answers, go back and underline all examples of comparatives and superlatives.

1 Which burns longer – a black candle or a white candle?
   > . . . .

2 What are you going to do when you are as big as your mother?
   > . . . .

3 Who is the strongest criminal?
   > . . . .

4 Have you heard that the most intelligent person in the world is going deaf?
   > . . . .

5 Why are wolves like playing cards?
   . . . .

6 What is worse than finding a worm in your apple?
   > . . . .

7 Indecisive Customer: I've changed my mind again.
   Irritated Shop Assistant: . . . .

8 How do you know when you are middle-aged?
   > . . . .

"Eeek!"

9 What is even harder than a diamond?
   > . . . .

A Finding half a worm.

B And is the new one working better than the old one?

C When the cake costs less than the candles.

D A shoplifter.

E Neither, they both burn shorter.

F Paying for it!

G Go on a diet.

H Pardon?

I They both come in packs.

14   Jokes with SO....THAT

All these jokes contain the structure *so ..... that.* What kind of words can follow *so?* How
many of these jokes can be re-written using *such* instead of *so?*

1   My father has so many gold teeth that . . . .

2   I was so big when I was born that . . . .

3   In Spain the melons are so big that . . . .

4   The people in my village talk so much that . . . .

5   The Megalith Hotel is so tall that . . . .

6   My sister is so thin that . . . .

7   Dolphins are so clever that . . . .

8   I have so many wrinkles on my forehead that . . . .

9   My hair is so wavy that . . . .

10 The holiday resort was so dull that . . . .

A   the ducks throw her bread when she goes to the park.

B   to call reception from the top floor you have to dial long distance.

C   the tide went out one day and never came back.

D   you can hollow them out and use them as houses.

E   they can train a man to stand on the edge of their pool and throw them fish
    three times a day.

F   he has to sleep with his head in a safe.

G   the doctor was afraid to slap me.

H   people get seasick looking at me.

I   they have to put sun cream on their tongues when they go on holiday.

J   I have to screw my hat on.

15   The Best Way

It is always too easy to look at the answers. Make sure you try to think of your OWN answer to each of these sentences first. Then compare your answers with those given.

1   The best way to meet a new neighbour is . . . .

2   The best way to cut your food bill in half is . . . .

3   The best way to get a seat on crowded buses is . . . .

4   The best way to turn people's heads is . . . .

5   The best way to catch a mouse is . . . .

6   The best way to light a fire with two sticks is . . . .

7   The best way to make a cigarette lighter is . . . .

8   The best way to stop a cockerel crowing on a Sunday is . . . .

9   The best way to cover an old cushion is . . . .

10   The best way to communicate with a fish is . . . .

A   to cook it on Saturday.

B   to take the tobacco out.

C   to drop it a line.

D   to use a pair of scissors.

E   to sit on it.

F   to enter the theatre after the show has begun.

G   to play loud music at 2 o'clock in the morning.

H   to become a driver.

I   to make sure one of them is a match.

J   to get somebody to throw you one.

16 Misunderstanding Grammar

We're having *my mother* for lunch. > Really, we're having *chicken*. – They have the same grammar, but the meanings are totally different. These jokes depend on this idea.

1 The police are looking for a man with one eye called Wilson.

> . . . .

2 I've been waiting here for five minutes to cross this road.
> Well, there's a zebra crossing further down the road.

> . . . .

3 Doctor: You must take one of these pills three times a day.
Patient: . . . .

4 I had to get up early this morning to open the door in my pyjamas.

> . . . .

5 William, run over and see how old Mrs Smith is.
(*William returns five minutes later.*)
> She's annoyed, mum. She said . . . .

6 Did you know that deep breathing kills germs?

> . . . .

7 Did you wake up grumpy this morning?

> . . . .

8 Your dog is chasing a man on a bicycle.

> . . . .

9 I've made the chicken soup.

> . . . .

A Oh good. I was afraid it was for us.

B Yes, but how do you get them to breathe deeply?

C it is none of your business how old she is.

D Don't be stupid. My dog can't cycle.

E What's the other eye called?

F No. I just let him sleep late.

G That's a strange place to have a door.

H How on earth can I take it more than once?

I Well, I hope it is having better luck than I'm having.

17 Questions with HOW

The answers to these questions are not the ones you would expect. When you have agreed the answers, discuss whether you can translate them into your language.

1 How can you divide seven potatoes equally between four people?
   > . . . .

2 How long will the next bus be?
   > . . . .

3 Inspector: How many people work in this office?
   Manager: . . . .

4 How much does it cost to get married, dad?
   > . . . .

5 How can you double your money?
   > . . . .

6 Headmaster: How can we raise the level of our students?
   Teacher: . . . .

7 How can you make eleven an even number?
   > . . . .

8 How do you stop fish from smelling?
   > . . . .

9 Well, Peter, how do you like school?
   > . . . .

10 How can you tell which end of a worm is its head?
   > . . . .

"Well, Peter, how do you like school?"

    A   Cut off their noses.
    B   About half of them.
    C   Remove the first two letters.
    D   I don't know. I'm still paying for it.
    E   Closed.
    F   We could use the upstairs classrooms.
    G   Tickle it in the middle and wait until it smiles.
    H   Mash them.
    I   About six metres.
    J   Look at it in a mirror.

18   Questions with WHY

After you have filled in the gaps correctly, think carefully about each answer. You may need a dictionary to discover why each is funny.

1   Why are false teeth like stars?
>   Because they both come out at . . . .

2   Why did the man with one hand cross the road?
>   To get to the . . . . shop.

3   Why is a banana like a jersey?
>   Because it's easy to . . . . on.

4   Why are cooks cruel?
>   Because they . . . . eggs,
    . . . . cream, and . . . . fish.

"Why are false teeth like stars?"

5   Why do teachers at university wear sunglasses?
>   Because their students are very . . . .

6   Why is it easy to weigh a fish as soon as you catch it?
>   Because it has its own . . . .

7   Why is a pocket calculator reliable?
>   Because you can always . . . . on it.

8   Why do cows wear bells?
>   In case their . . . . don't work.

9   Why is a room full of married people always empty?
>   Because there isn't a . . . . person in it.

10   Why did the nurse open the medicine cabinet quietly?
>   Because she didn't want to wake up the . . . .

horns	sleeping pills	scales
night	count	slip
single	second hand	bright
beat	whip	batter

19 Any Suggestions?

Do your best not to look at the answers to this lesson. Try to think of your OWN answers first, agree on them in class, and then see how close or far you were from the real ones!

1   Nobody ever complained about . . . . not opening.

2   My wife and I were happy for twenty years. Then we . . . .

3   Someone has invented a new alarm clock for actors. It doesn't ring, it . . . .

4   People with loud coughs never go to the doctor, they go to . . . .

5   Goldsmith's wife made him a millionaire. Before she married him, he was a . . . .

6   The only time I have trouble with anxiety is when I try to . . . .

7   I'm thinking of becoming a doctor. I have the . . . . for it.

8   I was so surprised at . . . . that I didn't talk for a year.

9   I decided to sell my drums when I saw my neighbour coming home with . . . .

10 Is another name for a funeral parlour a . . . . lounge?

An actors' alarm clock

A   handwriting

B   a shotgun

C   my birth

D   a parachute

E   applauds

F   spell it

G   met

H   the cinema

I   billionaire

J   departure

20 What's the Context?

Here are 8 sentences. What is the situation in each? When you have decided that, match them to the 8 situations below. Try first to guess the situation before looking at the dialogues.

1 Just a minute.
2 Should someone be punished for something they haven't done?
3 Have you seen her mother?
4 Do you know your house is on fire?
5 But I haven't done anything.
6 Certainly not. It wouldn't be right.
7 DOGS MUST BE CARRIED
8 No. I'm afraid I don't.

"I can't find one!"

A I'm afraid that I have to tell you that you're sacked.
   > . . . .
   That's why you've been fired.

B Mr Wilson, I'd like to ask for your permission to marry your daughter.
   > . . . .
   Yes, but I prefer your daughter.

C Could you help me with my homework?
   > . . . .
   Maybe not, but you could at least try!

D A man walked into a pub where a pianist was playing and said,
   " . . . . "
   "No," said the pianist, "But if you hum it I'll try to follow you."

E Late again. What's your excuse this time?
   > Sorry sir, but there was a notice on the bus saying . . . .
   and I couldn't find one anywhere.

F Sir, ...
   > No, of course not.
   Good, because I haven't done my homework.

G Do you know the way to the post office?
   > . . . .
   Well, go down this road and take the first turning on the left.

H A man wanted to travel from London to Hong Kong so he telephoned a travel agent to find out how long the flight was.
   " . . . ." said the agent.
   " Thank you very much," said the man and hung up.

21 Insulting Remarks

Some people are proud of being able to say things which are very clever and at the same time very insulting. All these jokes depend on this idea.

1   Will you love me when I'm old and ugly?
    > Of course, ...

2   Singer: Did you notice how my voice filled the hall?
    Critic: And did you notice . . . .

3   I'm not myself tonight.
    > Yes, ...

4   Teacher: What is wrong with saying 'I have went'?
    Student: . . . .

5   You remind me of the sea.
    > You mean, because I'm wild, reckless and romantic?
    . . . .

6   Father: Don't you think our son got his intelligence from me?
    Mother: He must have done. . . . .

7   I'm thirty-eight and I don't look it, do I?
    > No, ...

8   Very Fat Lady: I would like to see a dress that fits me.
    Shop Assistant: . . . .

9   I wish you and your rock group were on TV.
    > So you think we are that good!
    . . . .

A   I've still got mine.

B   So would I.

C   You are still here.

D   No, because then I could switch you off.

E   I do.

F   how the audience left to make room for it?

G   but you used to.

H   No, because you make me sick.

I   I've noticed the improvement.

22   Definitions

First, look at the nine words in the box at the bottom. Try to say what they mean without using a dictionary. Then match them to these definitions.

1   A/an . . . . is somebody who has stopped growing except around the waist.

2   A/an . . . . is somebody you know well enough to borrow money from, but not well enough to lend money to.

3   A/an . . . . is a set of holes tied together with string.

4   A/an . . . . is somebody whose career is in ruins.

5   A/an . . . . is something one generation buys, the next generation gets rid of, and the following generation buys again.

6   A piece of . . . . is something everybody gives but few take.

7   A/an . . . . is a mechanical device for waking up people who do not have children.

8   A/an . . . . is somebody who thinks twice before saying nothing.

9   . . . . is the only thing money can't buy.

antique	archaeologist	adult
diplomat	alarm clock	poverty
net	acquaintance	advice

23 Paradoxical Jokes

A paradox is when two things seem to contradict each other – *the comedian was so bad, he was almost good!* **All these jokes contain a paradox.**

1 What gets wet as it dries?

> . . . .

2 What has a bed but does not sleep? It also has a mouth but does not speak.

> . . . .

3 What can you look through but not see through?

> . . . .

4 What has teeth but can't bite?

> . . . .

5 What can you give somebody and still keep?

> . . . .

6 What has a neck but no head?

> . . . .

7 What runs but has no legs?

> . . . .

8 What can travel round the world yet stay in one corner?

> . . . .

9 What is black when it's clean and white when it's dirty?

> . . . .

a stamp	a towel	your word
a bottle	a blackboard	a book
a tap	a comb	a river

24 What's the Difference?

This is another typical type of joke in English. The answers always follow the same pattern –
One . . . . , the other . . . .

What is the difference between:

1   . . . . . . a lazy student and a fisherman?

2   . . . . . . a doormat and a bottle of medicine?

3   . . . . . . a hungry man and a greedy man?

4   . . . . . . a clothes brush and an iceberg?

5   . . . . . . a storm cloud and a child being spanked?

6   . . . . . . a farmer and a tailor?

7   . . . . . . a night watchman and a butcher?

8   . . . . . . a jeweller and a jailer?

9   . . . . . . a train driver and a teacher.

A   One longs to eat, the other eats too long.

B   One pours with rain, the other roars with pain.

C   One minds the train, the other trains the mind.

D   One is shaken up and taken, the other is taken up and shaken.

E   One gathers what he sows, the other sews what he gathers.

F   One sells watches, the other watches cells.

G   One hates his books, the other baits his hooks.

H   One brushes coats, the other crushes boats.

I   One stays awake, the other weighs a steak.

25 Waiter! Waiter!

Jokes involving complaints to waiters in restaurants are a classic kind of joke in English. Have you heard any which start – *Waiter! Waiter! There's a fly in my soup!*

1   Waiter: How did you find the steak, sir?
    Customer: ....

2   Customer: Waiter! This plate is wet.
    Waiter: ....

3   Customer: This soup tastes funny.
    Waiter: ....

4   Customer: Waiter! How long have you been working here?
    Waiter: Six months, sir.
    Customer: ....

5   Customer: Waiter! This lobster only has one claw.
    Waiter: I'm sorry, sir. It must have been in a fight.
    Customer: ....

6   Customer: I'll have a hamburger, please.
    Waiter: With pleasure.
    Customer: ....

"I'll have this one, thank you very much!"

7   Customer: Waiter! This meal isn't fit for a pig.
    Waiter: ....

8   Customer: Waiter! This coffee tastes like mud!
    Waiter: ....

9   Customer: I wish to complain about this food. Call the chef!
    Waiter: ....

A   No, with mustard and ketchup, please.
B   I'm afraid he's gone out for lunch.
C   Well, it was ground only a few minutes ago.
D   I'll take it away and bring you something that is, sir.
E   Well, it can't have been you who took my order.
F   Oh! I just moved the potato and there it was.
G   That's your soup, sir.
H   Then, bring me the winner!
I   Then, why aren't you laughing?

26   Doctor! Doctor!

Another classic type of joke in English involves a two-line conversation between a patient and a doctor. Do these exist in your language?

1   Patient: Doctor! Doctor! I think I'm getting smaller.

Doctor: ....

2   Patient: Doctor! Doctor! Everybody keeps ignoring me.

Doctor: ....

3   Patient: Is it serious, doctor?

Doctor: Well. ....

4   Doctor: Well, Mr Smith, you seem to be coughing much more easily this morning.

Patient: ....

5   Doctor: Are the pills I gave you to improve your memory helping you?

Patient: ....

6   Doctor: I have to tell you that you are seriously ill. Is there anything you would like?

Patient: ....

7   Patient: Doctor, please help me. I can't stop telling lies.

Doctor: ....

8   Doctor: I'm afraid the pain in your right arm is just old age.

Patient: ....

9   Patient: I feel like a pack of cards.

Doctor: ....

A   I wouldn't start watching any new television serials.

B   I don't believe you.

C   Well, you'll just have to learn to be a little patient.

D   Then why doesn't my left arm hurt? I've had it just as long.

E   Take a seat and I'll deal with you later.

F   That's because I've been practising all night.

G   Yes, a second opinion.

H   What pills?

I   Next please!

27 Making Fun of Teachers!

Teachers who ask questions which students can make fun of are the subject of these jokes. Do your best to think of your OWN answer first.

1   Teacher: Did your sister help you with your homework?
Student: No, ...

2   Teacher: George, name two pronouns in English?
George: . . . .
Teacher: Excellent! Well done.

3   Teacher: Elena, how do you spell wrong?
Elena: R O N G.
Teacher: . . . .
Elena: That's what you asked for, wasn't it?

4   Teacher: Klaus, can you tell me what the plural of 'baby' is?
Klaus: . . . .

5   Teacher: Irma, what is the most popular answer to questions asked by teachers?
Irma: . . . .
Teacher: Correct.

6   Teacher: (talking on the telephone) ..... So Gordon can't come to school because he has a cold. Who am I speaking to?
Voice: . . . .

7   Teacher: First there was the Ice Age, then the Stone Age. Paul, what came next?
Paul: . . . .

8   Teacher: Laura. Say something beginning with the letter 'I'.
Laura: I is .....
Teacher: No. No. No. You must say 'I am'.
Laura: Okay then. . . . .

9   Teacher: If you add 376 and 478, and divide the answer by 14, what do you get?
Student: . . . .

A   That's wrong.
B   I don't know.
C   I am the ninth letter of the alphabet.
D   The sausage?
E   The wrong answer.
F   Twins?
G   She did all of it.
H   Who, me?
I   This is my father.

28 Alphabet Jokes

Letters of the alphabet can also be words – Did U C the length of the Q! These jokes depend on this idea.

1 What letters of the alphabet are bad for your teeth?

> . . . .

2 What occurs once in every minute, twice in every moment but never in five hundred thousand years?

> . . . .

3 Why should you never put the letter M in the fridge?

> . . . .

4 What letters of the alphabet do athletes need?

> . . . .

5 Why is the letter E lazy?

> . . . .

6 When were there only three vowels in the alphabet?

> . . . .

7 What is the most unlucky letter in the alphabet?

> . . . .

8 What eight-letter word has only one letter in it?

> . . . .

9 Why is an island like the letter T?

> . . . .

10 Why is the letter C like a magician?

> . . . .

A   N-R-G.
B   Before U and I were born.
C   Envelope
D   It can turn ash into cash.
E   D-K.
F   It turns ice into mice.
G   It is always in the middle of water.
H   The letter M.
I   It is always in bed.
J   U because when there is trouble, you will always find U in the middle of it.

29 Elephant Jokes

Why do elephants paint their toe-nails pink? – So they can hide in cherry trees! This is the classic schoolboy's elephant joke. This might help you answer these questions!

1 How do you get four elephants in a car?

> . . . .

2 How can you tell that an elephant has been in the refrigerator?

> . . . .

3 What time is it when an elephant sits on your car?

> . . . .

4 What do you do if an elephant sneezes?

> . . . .

5 How do you stop an elephant going through the eye of a needle?

> . . . .

6 How do you know if there is an elephant under your bed?

> . . . .

7 Why is an elephant large, grey and wrinkled?

> . . . .

8 How does an elephant get down from a tree?

> . . . .

9 Why did the elephant decide to give up his job with the circus?

> . . . .

10 Why can't two elephants go into the swimming pool at the same time?

> . . . .

"How do you get ONE elephant in a car?"

A Get out of the way very quickly.

B Because if it was small, white and smooth it would be an aspirin.

C They only have one pair of trunks between them.

D Time to buy a new one.

E The ceiling is very close.

F Two in the front and two in the back.

G You can see its footprints in the butter.

H Tie a knot in its tail.

I It was tired of working for peanuts.

J It sits on a leaf and waits for autumn.

Section Two
Cartoons

This section consists of a number of cartoons where a problem-solving task is created by removing something from the original cartoon. The main aim of the design of the worksheet is to motivate the student to speak.

The worksheets are divided into three categories with three worksheets in each:

    1.   What's missing from the cartoon?
         – where words or objects have been removed.

    2.   What happens next?
         – where the final frame of the cartoon has been removed.

    3.   What's the caption?
         – where the caption or punchline has been removed.

Each worksheet is in two sections. The upper half sets the task and provides a number of questions which direct the students' attention to the missing element. The lower half provides the solution.

Procedure
You can fold the sheet or cut it up – depending on the maturity of your class!
Use the questions to focus on various aspects of the cartoon. Try to stimulate as much discussion as possible. Let the students work in pairs or in groups. Discuss the suggestions in a whole-class session. Only when you feel you have exhausted all the possibilities should you hand out / uncover the bottom half of the sheet.
You can then use your own favourite cartoons in a similar way.

How well do you know your road signs? This one is common in Britain. What do you think it means? Where would you see it? What do you think is written below the triangle?

Who is this man? Where is he? Why is he holding an atlas of the world? What is he looking at on the desk? What do you think is written on the object? Why is he looking puzzled?

What does the machine on the left measure? What does the middle machine measure? What is on top of the machine on the right? What do you think this machine measures?

Scott A. Masear

Why is the man begging? Who comes along? Does he give the man any money? What does he do to the man? Why do you think he did that?

Why do you think the fish are watching the man? Describe the look on their faces. What is sitting on the stool beside the fish tank? What kind of restaurant is this?

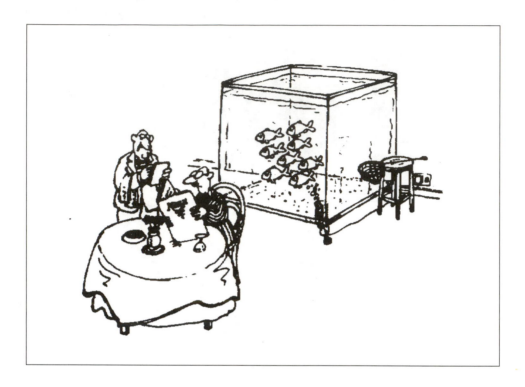

"I'll have the steak"

1. What is the man about to do?   2. What message does he get?
3. How does he react?   4. What will happen in number 4?

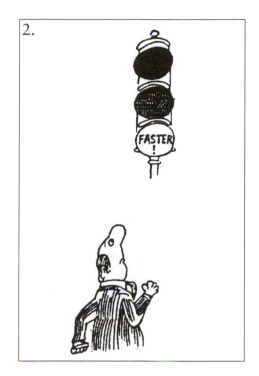

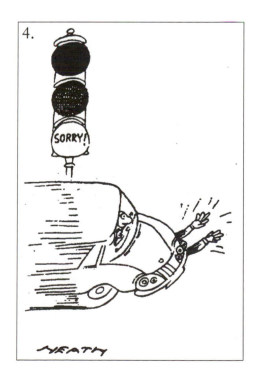

Where do these people live? What is the weather like there? What is wrong with the nose of the man on the right? How has this happened? What is his friend saying to him?

Bless you!

What kind of things has the man bought? How much will he have to pay? Why does he have to pay so much? What do you think the cashier is saying to him?

Are you sure your tie didn't flop over the bar-code scanner, sir?

What kind of place do you think this is? Why do people prefer these places to zoos? Why do the people stay in their cars? What is the lioness saying to her two cubs?

I think it's cruel the way they keep them cooped up in those little cages.

Section Three
Misprints

The worksheets in this section consist of a collection of short texts with misprints. Misprints occur relatively frequently in newspapers and magazines, and occasionally they have humorous consequences. The task of the student is to find the misprints and correct them, while enjoying the humour in the process. This is also a useful awareness-raising exercise and a useful way to focus students on the need to proof-read their own writing carefully.

This section consists of nine worksheets, loosely grouped according to level. The level is given in the top right-hand corner of each page like this:

       A for Elementary students
       B for Intermediate students
       C for Advanced students

This grading is not rigid and some worksheets will be appreciated by a range of levels.

Each worksheet consists of ten short texts and a cartoon. All the texts on a worksheet have the same type of misprint. The cartoon shows the type of misprint on that particular worksheet. At each level there are three types.

       A word with **the wrong letter**
       A word with **a missing letter**
       A word with **an extra letter**

Procedure
Hand out a worksheet and ask students to look at the cartoon. Get them to try to explain the situation depicted. It will be difficult to find a reasonable explanation. Now get the students to read the text on the right of the cartoon. The students should be able to locate the word in the text which is problematic and suggest what it should be. For example, in the introductory text to Lesson 39 the word 'mule' should be 'male'. This now solves the problem created by the cartoon.

Explain to the students that the remaining nine texts on the worksheet have misprints of the same type and ask them to find them. This is best done in groups. The teacher might want to exploit the vocabulary in the texts either during the setting up, or after the completion of the activity.

A productive exercise can follow in which students write their own texts with misprints and pass them to others in the class to read.

Each text on this page contains a mistake where one letter in a word is wrong. For example, if the word should be *hat*, perhaps it is printed as *hot*.

"Will you marry me?"

1.

LONELY HEARTS

Small, single, intelligent woman wishes to meet tall, attractive, non-smoking mule. Please send photos and phone number to Box 242.

2.

ARIES (Mar 21 - Apr 20)

This is an important week for you. You will meet somebody who can change your wife. Listen carefully and many of your problems will go away and this will be a happy time for you.

3.

Relax in the quiet atmosphere of

HARRY'S BAR

Meals served in the restaurant from
12.00 - 2.30
and
5.00 to 11.00
Bad snacks served all day

4.

SMITH SENT OFF

Bobby Smith, the English international footballer, was sent off during a match against Germany. The referee showed Smith the red card after he licked the German goalkeeper in the last minute of the game.

5.

46, High St. Small comfortable flat for sale in the town centre. One bedroom, large kitchen, and loving-room. Suit young couple with no children. £45,000 o.n.o. Visiting Sat & Sun 2.00 - 4.00pm.

6.

BOEING'S NEW PLANT WILL CARRY 800 PASSENGERS

7.

Dear Juliet,
I must see you as soon as possible or I will go mad. Please meet me outside the cinema on Saturday night at six. I don't want there to be any trouble, so sell your parents before you come.
Much love,
Romeo

8.

TELEVISION

3.05 The secret life of plants.
3.30 Football. Ajax v Liverpool
6.00 News followed by News for the dead.
6.20 Weather
6.30 The Natural World: Food from the sea.

9.

A seven-year-old boy got a free trip to America last month, on the Queen Elizabeth II, one of the world's largest chips. He didn't have a ticket but he told a member of the crew that his parents were on the boat and they had his ticket and passport.

10.

HOLIDAY of a LIFETIME

**Get close to nature.
Sleep under the stars.
Eat outside at an open fire.
Go where you like.
Hire a cat to take you into the jungle.
Photograph wild animals.**

Phone 1221 443 4567

Each text on this page contains a mistake where one letter in a word is missing. For example, if the word should be *hate*, perhaps it is printed as *hat*.

"Thank goodness I didn't lose my brushes!"

1.
Artist, Pablo Cassels, lost his pants on the London Underground last week and he has offered £200 to the person who returns them. Pablo was travelling on the Circle Line from 3.00 to 3.30 p.m. on Thursday the 26th. If you have any information, phone 0178 3345656.

2.
TEST IN ENGLISH
(1hr 45mins)
ANSWER BOOKLET

Please read the instructions very carefully.
Answer all questions in black ink.
Lose your answer booklet when the examiner tells you.

3.
Very young children will pick up insects and they will even try to eat them. It is important that parents teach their children about the different kinds of insect. For example, it is important they know that bees sing when they are touched.

4.
ZOO ATTACK
Police are looking for a man who attacked a young girl in the city zoo. The police now have a photofit picture of the man. He is in his 30s, tall, with blond hair, and a brown bear. He was wearing a blue and white jacket at the time of the attack.

5.
Newcastle is a city in the north of England. It has a population of 200,000 people. It has a university, a cathedral and one of the largest hopping centres in the world, the Metro Centre. People from Newcastle have a special name. They are called 'Geordies'.

6.
OLYMPIC SHOCK

**CHRISTIE
EATS
LEWIS
IN 100 METRE
FINAL**

7.
Wilson Wynott, the director of the giant Ford motor company, had a heart attack yesterday. He is now recovering in hospital but doctors think that he will be able to return to work next week. Thousands of Ford workers have sent get-well cars to their boss.

8.
TAYLOR UNHAPPY

Peter Ferguson, manager of Colchester United Football club, has decided not to pay the team's top goal scorer, Mark Taylor, because he has a bad cold. Mr Taylor said that he was not happy and that he might ask for a transfer.

9.
Tourists come to London to visit the historic buildings, such as the Houses of Parliament, where you can see and hear the famous lock, Big Ben. They also come to visit its theatres, museums and shops, such as the world-famous Harrods, where you can buy anything.

10.
ICE STARS ARRIVE
Competitors from all over the world are arriving in Ottawa, Canada, for the World Ice-Dancing Championships.
Many people think the British will win because they have the strongest tea.

Each text on this page contains a mistake where a word has an extra letter. For example, if the word should be *war*, perhaps it is printed as *wart*.

"Cheers!"

1.

TWENTY-TWO PEOPLE BECOME ILL AFTER DRINKING THE WAITER AT A CITY CENTRE RESTAURANT

2.

Dear Swee Ho,
I am very pleased to hear that you are enjoying your studies in England. Remember that winter is cold there so make sure you put lots of clothes on. I hope you see some snow.
Auntie Joyce sends her glove.
Love,
Mum

3.

ST MARK'S CHURCH

SUMMER FUND-RAISING SALE IN CHURCH HALL

15th July 3.00 p.m.
£1
Pray as you enter

4.

Helen Collins, the film star, became ill while she was having her hair cut at a London salon yesterday. The hairdresser took Miss Collins outside to get some fresh hair and she soon felt better. She returned to the salon and told reporters later that she was pleased with her new style.

5.

HOTEL PARADISE

* 186 comfortable rooms
* all with TV and telephone
* good views of the seat
* 2 restaurants
* 24-hr room service
* 20 mins. from the airport
* parking for 200 cars
* reasonable prices

6.

LARGE OFFICE

TOILET

1000 sq metres
£2000 per month

Phone 0131 445 6464

7.

A SIMPLE PASTA SAUCE
1. Finely chop two onions.
2. Crush two cloves of garlic.
3. Put some soil in a pot and heat it gently.
4. Add the onion and garlic and fry for three minutes.
5. Add a tin of chopped tomatoes and heat for two minutes, then serve.

8.

General Otode, the leader of the world's smallest country, lost his army in a terrible car crash last week. The general is now in the main hospital. Doctors said that he was extremely shocked and unable to talk.

9.

TO USE THE PHONE

1. Lift handset.
2. Insert monkey.
3. Dial number and wait for the connection.
4. Replace handset when your call is finished.

10.

In England the number of people going to church is going down and down. As a result, over a thousand churches had to close last year. A church leader said that more and more people were now looking for gold outside the church.

Each text on this page contains a mistake where one letter in a word is wrong. For example, if the word should be *hat*, perhaps it is printed as *hot*.

"He's scored!"

1.
Two minutes from the end of the match Edwards scored his first goal for his country. The tall blind player from Swansea, playing in only his second game for Wales, went past three English players before putting the ball past the goalkeeper into the net.

2.
LUCKY ESCAPE
A motorist had a remarkable escape yesterday when his car left the road during a violent thunderstorm and crashed into a tree. Peter Burgess said that a combination of wet roads and strong wines had caused him to lose control of the car.

3.
At dawn a small group of fishermen gathered outside government offices to protest against the plans to restrict fishing in the North Sea. The crowd soon began to smell and by noon it had brought traffic in the area to a standstill.

4.
6.00 FARMING WORLD
The programme examines how labour-saving machinery like tractors, chemical fertilizers, and pesticides have helped the modern farmer to harm the land more efficiently and effectively in the twentieth century.

5.
Everything in nature is recycled. Animal and vegetable remains feed the soil, which nourishes new life. The concept of rubbish is a very decent idea peculiar to modern man. Britain produces 20 million tonnes of rubbish from houses, shops and offices every year.

6.
MOBILE HOLE FOR SALE
On a select site overlooking Dorset Bay modern, furnished, sleeps 6

Phone 0145 557744

7.
The development of the Space Shuttle has dramatically reduced the cost of sending satellites into space. The Shuttle takes off like a rocket but lands like an ordinary plane. It can be used time and time again. The Shuttle's large cargo-hold is capable of carrying huge toads into space.

8.
Twenty-six passengers were treated for shock at a hospital in London yesterday after receiving slight injuries as they slid down the emergency escape chutes from a Pan Am jumbo jet at Heathrow Airport. The chutes were activated by a faulty switch on the fright deck.

9.
SUCCESSFUL businessman, widower, aged 44, non-smoker with varied interests seeks affectionate, understanding female to shave the enjoyable things in life.
Box No. 4881,
Yorkshire Post Ltd.
Leeds 1.

10.
A young woman was arrested last night in connection with the theft of a £150,000 fur coat from a Paris boutique. The coat has been returned to the owners. The woman was naked this morning. Police identified her as Jill Young from Bristol, England. Young said she stole the coat as a protest against the fur trade.

Each text on this page contains a mistake where one letter in a word is missing. For example, if the word should be *hate*, perhaps it is printed as *hat*.

"Stay indoors!"

1.

Leo the Lion escaped from Chesterfield Zoo last night. There have been a number of sightings of Leo by people living near the zoo. A team of zoo-keepers are following Leo's tail and they are confident that they will recapture him quickly. The public are advised to stay indoors.

2.

Celebrate Christmas
in the heat
of Scotland at
THE BRAEMAR INN
3 days from £120 f.b.
traditional fare and
entertainment
superb skating and skiing
facilities nearby.
Tel: (01468) 23434

3.

The River Oxen burst its banks after three days of heavy rain. A wave of water one metre high swept across fields of wheat, corn and vegetables before it hit the village of Crindle. The villagers were unprepared and three people were killed by the food.

4.

HOLIDAY ADVICE

1. Always pack a small first-aid kit.
2. If you are bitten by an animal, go to a doctor or hospital.
3. Make sure the drinking water is safe. If you are not sure, boil the water or use sterilization tables.

5.

Eighty-year-old Mrs Helen Warren was recovering from shock and cold yesterday after spending six hours in a park terrorised by a dog. Mrs Warren said that the dog approached her as she sat on a park bench. At first the dog seemed friendly, but when it started to grow she was too afraid to move.

6.

TEENAGER KILLS

TEN CLASSMATES

WITH SHOTGUN

AFTER WATCHING

VIOLET TV FILMS

7.

Four hundred years ago there were about six million English speakers in the world. Today there are over 350 million people who use English as their other tongue, and about one billion people who use English as a foreign language.

8.

**HEAD WAITER
WANTED FOR
FIVE-STAR HOTEL**

Experience essential, with a good knowledge of food and beverages. The successful applicant will have a smart appearance and peasant manners. 40 hrs /wk. Excellent salary.

9.

Ray Hardy, the popular British chef, has had his cooking equipment stolen. When asked about his future pans, Mr Hardy said that he would probably buy from Harrods in London but nothing could really replace the original equipment, some of which he has had since he was a trainee chef.

10.

RAIN STOPS ROCKET

Four hundred VIPs were disappointed after the lunch date of the Ariane space rocket had to be postponed due to bad weather. A spokesman said that the next suitable date would be in three weeks' time.

Each text on this page contains a mistake where a word has an extra letter. For example, if the word should be *war*, perhaps it is printed as *wart*.

"Quick thinking, boy!"

1.

Fire broke out last night, in the stables of the millionaire racehorse owner, the Aga Khan. A quick-thinking stableboy prevented any serious damage from being done by grabbing a nearby horse and extinguishing the blaze.

2.

The Minister of Education said that it was obvious to everybody that school-children today have to learn much more than their parents had to. As a result, the Minister told reporters that the Government was now considering an increase in the school-leaving wage.

3.

**John Kilroy Keyes
1923-1995**

John passed away peacefully yesterday after a short illness. For forty years he was an enthusiastic teacher of Physics at Oxford University. He will be remembered by his students around the world. He leaves a son and a window.

4.

45 guerrillas walked out of the jungle yesterday and surrendered to government troops. They were taken to the presidential palace, where a lavish meal had been prepared for them. Most of the guerrillas said they considered the meal a threat after spending so many years preparing their own food.

5.

VIRGO
(24 Aug - 22 Sept)

This is not a week to be sociable. Somebody is jealous of you. Do not travel. Stay at home if you can. Avoid meetings with stranglers. A week to be careful, but don't despair, your luck will change next week.

6.

**ENGLISH STUDY
TOURS   PLC**

GHOST FAMILIES
WANTED FOR YOUNG
ITALIAN STUDENTS ON
SUMMER COURSES

£100 per week B&B
Phone 0131 334 56544

7.

BOSS SECURITY

require strong, young men for crowd control duties at pop concerts around the country this summer. Martial Arts training an advantage. Scar essential.

Apply in writing to
Box No 243
including photograph.

8.

**Enthusiastic young person wanted for top London night sport. Must be fit. No experience needed, training provided. Uniform supplied. Good pay and prospects.
For further details phone:
0131 445 6767**

9.

**COME TO
SUNNY MAJORCA**

Majorca is the largest of the Balearic Islands, which live close to the south-east coast of Spain. The island's many fine beaches and its exciting night-life have made it one of the most popular holiday resorts in the world.

10.

One of Britain's largest holiday companies receives thousands of complaints from holidaymakers each year. Ron Old, head of customer relations, said that many of these complaints were about pretty little things that have little effect on the holiday-maker's overall enjoyment of their holiday.

Each text on this page contains a mistake where one letter in a word is wrong. For example, if the word should be *hat*, perhaps it is printed as *hot*.

"Trying to resolve the issue!"

1.

LAND DISPUTE HALTS NEW ROAD

A number of site owners are standing out against the council's decision to issue compulsory purchase orders on their land and a public inquiry will be held in Manchester on October 23 in a bed to resolve the issue.

2.

SEARCH ABANDONED

Police at Peebles yesterday called off a search for a 20-year-old woman who is believed to have frowned after falling into the swollen River Tweed. Belinda Lubbock had been receiving treatment for depression.

3.

PUTTENHAM, Florence. Late of 153 Henton Road, Colchester. A simple, kind and loving old lady who died with great dignity at 'Amblepark', Colchester, April 4, at 3.10pm. Loved by family and friends who knew her will.

4.

NO BACKING FOR STRIKE

While sympathising with the miners and arguing that the British government could have acted to end the strike, Jessica Larive Groenendaal said she and her Liberal colleagues could not support a strike called without a ballet.

5.

A large group of protesters against the new British immigration laws will hand over a petition to the British authorities today. The march will proceed from St. Stephen's Green to Simonscourt Road and a small delegation will be deceived at the British Embassy.

6.

HEART-LUNG
SWAP
WOMAN ON
MENU

7.

Bryan Hamilton, the Ipswich player, scored the goal, the headed pass being supplied by club colleague Allan Hunter. The 28,000 crows gave the team a moving ovation at the end of the match, evidence of how welcome football is at Windsor Park.

8.

MAN RUNS AMOK

A man who went berserk after being told that he was banned from a pub caused damage estimated at £1000.
Elliot Lamb (44) threw his glass at the bottles behind the bar. When the owner went to calm the police, Lamb destroyed bar fittings and upturned tables.

9.

International Topics is a book which provides text-based language practice at an upper intermediate level. It exposes the learner to expensive reading texts which present issues of current international interest, including technology, travel, the environment, sport and commerce.

10.

11:00 - 21 Days (film)
Larry accompanies Wanda, a mannequin with whom he is in love, to her apartment. There Wanda is met by Walley, her husband from whom she had parted several years previously. Walley attempts to blackmail Wanda and in a souffle, Larry accidentally kills him.

Each text on this page contains a mistake where one letter in a word is missing. For example, if the word should be *hate*, perhaps it is printed as *hat*.

"I'm just dying of hunger!"

1.
During the month of June, the Edinburgh Steak bar will be supporting the Mayor's appeal for a £450,000 brain scanner for the Southern General Hospital. For every customer who dies in the restaurant during the month, 20 pence will be donated towards the fund.

2.

THE CLEVELAND ARMS
resents entertainment
by
BOBBY RAY
On Saturday, March 23
Meals always available.

**Telephone
High Ercall 770204**

3.

TRAFFIC JAM
Commuters in Manchester faced a frustrating time getting to work yesterday. At one point traffic tailed back for five miles from the Salford junction where a bride is being re-painted.

4.

JUDO CLUB PRAISED FOR COMMUNITY SERVICE

Members of the judo club were congratulated by Peter White for the work their movement does to help disable people in the local community.

5.
Yesterday we were the guests of David Hessayon, the author of those slim but useful and beautifully illustrated booklets in the **Be Your Own Gardening Expert** series. They are cheap, brisk, down-to-earth guides on what to do in the garden, particularly on how to recognise pets and eliminate them.

6.

London Borough of HARROW

VOTE for improved health
Join our
ANT-SMOKING CLINIC

Write to the
Director of Health Services
Hanover House
Harrow.

7.
Harry Bull, 35, of Brighton Rd, Norwich, was already on bail after being arrested while trying to smuggle morphine through London Docks from India, said Mr David Calder, prosecuting. Bull was jailed for six years after admitting evading drug import regulations, burglary and reckless diving.

8.

SITUATIONS WANTED
Recently retired 70-year-old rusty messenger seeks part-time post in the City. Fit, healthy, reliable, adaptable with years of experience. Can start immediately, has own transport.

9.
If the Liberal party, which recently hanged its leader in an attempt to appeal to big business and the self-employed, fails to reach 5 per cent in the election, the Prime Minister may be forced to call off his alliance with the party.

10.

THE BRITISH JUNIOR SCHOOL, ATHENS
The school is now registering for all classes.
The curriculum prepares students for entry to the British Academy, teaching an English curriculum and including a full Greek curse if required.

Each text on this page contains a mistake where a word has an extra letter. For example, if the word should be *war*, perhaps it is printed as *wart*.

"We're hopping mad!"

1.

CHURCH PROTESTS

NEW YORK: A Roman Catholic bishop joined a group of Orthodox Jewish rabbits in condemning the 'Life of Brian,' a movie that they say is bigoted, blasphemous and a crime.

2.

Last night the boxing world welcomed the return of Mike Powers, now 40. Against all odds he ended the undefeated record of Joe Junior with a knockout in the tenth round. Mike Powers said that being the underdog always brings out the beast in him. He now hopes for a shot at the world title.

3.

STRESSED?
Take the Alternative approach.
Aromatherapy, Massage, Yoga, Acupuncture, Reflexology.
All our therapists are strained and experienced.

Tel: 0331 234 123

4.

With an ever-increasing awareness of healthy eating habits, more and more people are demanding cleaner meat from their butchers. The Minister of Health, John Wilson, said this was a welcome trend and that the government was keen to encourage its growth.

5.

Fun-loving male, 23, tall, slimy and intelligent, seeks warm, attractive woman for genuine friendship and lasting relationship. Non-smoker, professional with own home.
Box No 445

6.

ABRASIVE MEETINGS
a book by
V.S. ELIOT

WINNER OF THE 1992 TATE PRIZE FOR FRICTION

hardback edition - £12.00

7.

A young couple were fighting for their lives in the Royal Infirmary after being struck down by the deadly E-coli bacteria. Hygiene experts later discovered the source of the bacteria in a discarded cartoon at the couple's flat.

8.

Arsonists are believed to have started the fire which razed the one hundred and sixty year old wooden clubhouse of the Kent Cricket Club to the ground last night. At the site this morning club officials managed to find some of their precious silverware among the dying members.

9.

JAPANESE TRAVEL STRIKE ENDS
Japan's biggest transport strike ended early today after government meditation. Representatives from both sides of the dispute sat down with government officials late last night and reached a settlement after five hours.

10.

Nick Leeson, the high-flying investment manager with Barings Bank in Singapore, whose speculating on the international money markets bankrupted the bank, has been arrested in Germany. One furious director, on hearing of the bank's crippling losses, referred to Leeson as a bright idiot.

Section Four
Reading for Fun

This section consists of short amusing stories. The humour in these texts depends on the final line of the text. This has been removed to provide a problem-solving framework and a motivation for reading. Many of the texts also involve an element of repetition which provide the student with useful clues to the missing expression.

The worksheets are divided into three groups according to level. The level is given in the top right-hand corner of each page like this:

> A for Elementary students
>
> B for Intermediate students
>
> C for Advanced students

This grading is not rigid and most of the lessons will be appreciated by a range of levels.

Procedure

Allow the students to read a worksheet and deal with new vocabulary when it is considered necessary. Teachers can decide to exploit vocabulary during or after the activity of completing the task. Check comprehension of the text, then get the students to suggest what the final line or expression is. It is a good idea to let students do this in groups. When they have shared and evaluated their responses, reveal the final expression. It is useful to have this written somewhere, for example – on the reverse side of the blackboard – so that you can reveal it with dramatic effect.

Students now have a selection of humorous stories which they can tell to their friends outside class. Again this generates a natural form of language practice.

Can you guess the last line of this story?

An American architect was visiting London. He was on a business trip but he also wanted to see all the famous buildings in London. The American did not have much time so he stopped a taxi and asked the driver to take him to all the old and famous buildings in London.

The taxi driver drove him to the Tower of London.

"This is the Tower of London. It was a prison in the old days," he said.

The American looked at the building and said,

"It is so small. In America we could build this in a day."

The taxi driver took the American to Westminster Abbey. He said,

"This is a famous church. Kings and queens get married here."

The American looked at the old building and said,

"Huh. In America we could build this church in two days."

The driver decided to take the American to a bigger church so he drove him to St Paul's Cathedral. He stopped outside the church and said,

"This is the most famous church in England. The great architect Christopher Wren built this church."

The American got out of the taxi and looked at the church.

"Huh. In America we could build this church in three days," he said.

Next the driver took the American to the Houses of Parliament.

"This is where British politicians meet."

"Huh," the American said. "We could build this in four days."

The driver drove past Buckingham Palace, the home of Queen Elizabeth. As the taxi passed the palace, the American said,

"Hey. What is this big and beautiful building?"

The taxi driver looked at the palace and said,

" . . . . "

49   Boys and Girls

Can you guess the last line of this story?

Amanda Gardener was eighteen. Her parents decided to have her birthday party in a hotel. About two hundred people came to the party.

An old woman was staying in the hotel. She heard the music and came into the party room. The young boys and girls were dancing in the middle of the room. The old lady sat down and watched. Then she said,

"When I was young, parties were different. It was very easy to tell who was a boy and who was a girl. Today it is very difficult to tell who is a boy and who is a girl."

The person sitting next to her said nothing. The old lady continued,

"When I was young, boys wore trousers and girls wore dresses. Look at that girl over there. She's wearing boy's jeans."

The person sitting next to her said nothing. The old lady continued,

"When I was young, boys had short hair and girls had long hair, so it was very easy to tell who was a boy and who was a girl. That girl's hair is very short. It is a boy's haircut."

The person sitting next to her said nothing. Then the old lady said,

"Do you think she is a boy or a girl? It is very difficult to tell, isn't it?"

The person sitting next to her said,

"No. It is very easy for me because that girl is my daughter."

The old lady was very embarrassed and she said,

"Oh dear. I'm sorry. I didn't know you were her father."

The person sitting next to her replied,

" . . . . "

50   The Chauffeur

Can you guess the last line of this story?

Mrs Winterly was a very rich woman. Her husband was a multi-millionaire. She was quite young but he was quite old. She was twenty-eight. He was fifty-eight. They lived in a very large house in England.

Mrs Winterly never cooked or cleaned the house. She never worked and she never drove a car. When she wanted to go anywhere she would call Charles. Charles was her chauffeur.

Mr Winterly travelled a lot. He flew to many countries to do business. Mrs Winterly did not like to fly so she often stayed at home. Once Mr Winterly went to America for a week. Mrs Winterly decided to go shopping so she walked to the garage to find Charles. She found him in his room above the garage. Mrs Winterly looked at him and said,

"Charles. Take off my hat."

"Certainly, madam," Charles replied.

Then he took off Mrs Winterly's hat.

"Charles. Take off my coat."

"Certainly, madam," Charles replied.

Then he took off Mrs Winterly's coat.

"Charles. Take off my shoes."

"Certainly, madam," Charles replied.

Then he took off Mrs Winterly's shoes.

"Charles. Take off my dress."

"Certainly, madam," Charles replied.

Then he took off Mrs Winterly's dress.

Mrs Winterly looked into the eyes of her chauffeur and said,

" . . . . "

Can you guess the last line of this story?

One Sunday a young father was walking through the park. He was pushing a pram.

There was a very young baby in the pram and it was crying loudly. The young father

said softly,

"Take it easy, Martin. Keep calm, Martin. Control yourself, Martin."

The young father walked on but the child cried louder. The father stopped and took a

teddy bear out of a bag. He gave it to the child. He said softly,

"Take it easy, Martin. Keep calm, Martin. Control yourself, Martin."

The young father started to push the pram again. After a few minutes the child began

to cry. It cried louder and louder. The father put his hand into his pocket and took out

some chocolate. He gave a piece to the child and said softly,

"Take it easy, Martin. Keep calm, Martin. Control yourself, Martin."

The young father walked on. Three minutes later the child started to cry. It cried

louder and louder and louder. The father took the baby out of the pram and held it in

his arms. He said softly,

"Take it easy, Martin. Keep calm, Martin. Control yourself, Martin."

The child did not stop crying. It cried louder and louder.

An old woman was watching the father. She walked across to the young father and she

smiled. She said,

"You are doing very well, young man. You talk to the child with a calm and quiet

voice." The old woman looked at the child and said,

"What's wrong, Martin? Why are you crying?"

The father said quickly,

" . . . . "

Can you guess the last line of this story?

Linda Robinson was very thirsty so she went into a café. There was an old woman in the café. She was sitting at a table near the door. At her feet, under the table, there was a small dog. Linda bought a large glass of lemonade and some biscuits. She sat down at the table next to the old woman. The old woman sat quietly. She looked lonely. Linda decided to talk to the old woman. She said,

"It is very hot today."

"Yes, but it is nice and cool inside the café," replied the old woman.

Linda looked at the little dog and she asked,

"Does your dog like people?"

"Oh, he is very friendly."

Linda wanted to give the dog one of her biscuits so she asked,

"Does your dog like biscuits?"

"They are his favourite food," said the old woman.

Linda was afraid of dogs so she said,

"Does your dog bite?"

The old woman laughed and said,

"No. My dog is very tame. He is afraid of cats."

Linda took a biscuit from her plate and she put it near the dog's mouth. However, the dog didn't bite the biscuit, it bit Linda's hand. Linda jumped out of the chair and screamed in pain. In an angry voice, she shouted at the old woman,

"You said that your dog didn't bite."

The old woman looked at Linda and at the dog. Then she said,

"..."

Can you guess the last line of this story?

George was sitting in his English class. It was a hot afternoon and he was feeling sleepy. It was a grammar lesson and George was also bored. He hated grammar. He wanted to leave school and work. He wanted to be a gardener. George loved flowers and trees. George looked out of the window. He looked at the trees and flowers. Then he started day-dreaming.

After ten minutes the teacher stopped talking. She asked the students to do a grammar exercise in their books. The students took out their exercise books and their pencils and they started writing. The teacher looked at George. She saw that he wasn't writing so she said,

"Why aren't you writing, George?"

George stopped dreaming and said,

"What, Miss?"

"Wake up, George!" the teacher said. "Why aren't you writing?"

George thought for a moment and replied,

"I ain't got no pencil."

The teacher looked at George and said,

"You ain't got no pencil? You mean. I don't have a pencil."

George did not understand the English teacher so he said,

"Sorry, Miss."

The teacher said in an angry voice,

"I don't have a pencil. You don't have a pencil. He doesn't have a pencil. She doesn't have a pencil. We don't have pencils. They don't have pencils. Now, George. Do you understand?"

George looked at the teacher for a moment and then he said,

" . . . . "

Can you guess the last line of this story?

Allison Lumsden lived by herself in a small house. One day she received a letter. When she opened the letter there was a cinema ticket inside. There was also a note in the letter. It said,

'Here is a free ticket to the cinema on Saturday night. Enjoy yourself.'

However there was no name with the letter. Allison decided to telephone her friends to find out who sent her the present. First of all she called her father.

"Dad. Did you send me a cinema ticket?"

"No," he replied. "Perhaps it was your brother."

Allison called her brother.

"Andrew. Did you send me a cinema ticket?"

"No," he replied. "Perhaps it was Roberta."

Roberta was Allison's best friend so she rang her.

"Roberta. Did you send me a cinema ticket?"

"No," she replied.

Allison phoned all her friends but none of them had sent her the ticket. She decided to phone the manager of the cinema.

"My name is Allison Lumsden. I received a free ticket for your cinema on Saturday night. Did you send it to me?"

"No," said the manager.

Allison was puzzled. On Saturday night she did not know what to do but then she decided to use the ticket. She put on her coat and went to the cinema. It was a good film and she enjoyed herself. When she got home she was very surprised. There was a note on the front door of her house. It said,

" . . . . "

Can you guess the last line of this story?

A Frenchman, an Englishman and a German were travelling in a boat from France to Australia. Unfortunately, the boat sank but the three men swam to a small island. There was nobody on the island and it was thousands of kilometres from Australia. The men waited for another boat to come but none came. After two months they were very unhappy.

"We will have to live here forever," said the Englishman.

"We will have to eat bananas every day," said the German.

"We will never see our families again," said the Frenchman.

One day the German found an old bottle on the beach. He took the bottle to his two friends. When he opened the bottle a genie came out. The genie said to the three men, "Thank you for letting me out of the bottle. I was inside that bottle for five hundred years. Now I am free. I can give you two wishes each."

The German said,

"I am hungry and thirsty. I want some sausage to eat and some beer to drink. Secondly, I want to go back to Germany."

"Your wishes are granted," said the genie.

Five seconds later the German disappeared.

Next the Frenchman said,

"I am hungry and thirsty. I want some cheese to eat and some wine to drink. Secondly I want to return to my family in France."

"Your wishes are granted," said the genie.

Five seconds later the Frenchman disappeared.

"And what do you want?" the genie said to the Englishman.

The Englishman thought for a few minutes. Then he said,

".."

Can you guess the last line of this story?

Richard Sinclair worked for a zoo. He was a hunter. When the zoo wanted new animals, Richard went out and caught them. He was a very good hunter and he had an unusual way of catching animals.

One year the zoo needed some African tree monkeys so Richard went to Africa to catch some. He took a new assistant with him. Richard also took a very large dog with him. It was an angry dog and it had very large, sharp teeth. It often bit people so Richard tied a piece of rope around the dog's mouth to keep it closed.

The three of them travelled to Africa. They went into the jungle to an area where the tree monkeys lived. When they saw a tree monkey in a tall tree in front of them, Richard took out a large bag and a gun. He gave them to the assistant.

"What will I do with these?" the assistant asked.

"Listen carefully," Richard said. "I will climb the tree. Then I will shake the tree very hard and a monkey will fall out of it."

The assistant thought for a minute. Then he said,

"But the monkey is very fast and it will run away before I can catch it."

"Don't worry," Richard replied. "Take the rope from the dog's mouth. It is very angry and very fast. It will catch the monkey and bite it with its sharp teeth. The dog will hold the monkey in its mouth. You follow the dog and put the monkey in the bag. Very easy. Very simple and it works every time. Do you understand what to do?"

The assistant thought for a few seconds. Then he said,

"Yes. I understand what to do. But what do I need the gun for?"

Richard smiled and said,

" . . . . "

Can you guess the last line of this story?

One day a young lion walked through the jungle. He was young, strong and proud. The lion met a snake and said,

"Snake. Who is the king of the jungle?"

"You are," the snake replied quickly. It did not want to make the lion angry. The lion smiled and walked on. Thirty metres later he met a monkey. The lion looked at the monkey and said,

"Monkey. Who is the king of the jungle?"

"You are," the monkey replied. It turned round quickly and climbed a tree. It felt safe there. The lion looked up at the monkey and smiled. A few minutes later he met a crocodile. He stopped and said,

"Crocodile. Who is the king of the jungle?"

"You are," answered the crocodile. It went quickly into the river where it felt safe. The lion smiled and walked on. Next he met a giraffe. He looked up and shouted,

"Giraffe. Who is the king of the jungle?"

The giraffe did not answer so the lion roared loudly. The giraffe was very afraid and said, "You are."

"Answer quickly next time," said the lion, "or I might have to eat you." The lion walked on. He was very happy that all the other animals were afraid of him. A few hundred metres later he met an elephant.

"Elephant. Who is the king of the jungle?"

The elephant looked at the lion. Suddenly it picked the lion up with its trunk and dropped it on the ground. Next the elephant jumped on top of the lion. The lion was very surprised. Now it was dirty and hurt. It shouted at the elephant,

" . . . . "

Can you guess the last line of this story?

Andrew Wilson was visiting a home for old people. He went up to an old man who
had a very long white beard and said,

"Can I ask how old you are, sir?"

"Ninety-six," replied the old man.

"Why do you think you have lived so long?" asked Andrew.

"I don't smoke. I don't drink beer or wine."

At the other side of the room Andrew saw a man who looked older. He went up to the
man and asked politely,

"Can I ask how old you are, sir?"

"Ninety-nine," replied the old man.

"Why do you think you have lived so long?" asked Andrew.

"I don't smoke or drink. And I am not married," he said.

A nurse came into the room. She was pushing a very, very old man in a wheelchair.
Andrew said to the man,

"Can I ask how old you are, sir?"

"One hundred and ten years old," replied the old man.

"Why do you think you have lived so long?" asked Andrew.

"I don't smoke or drink. I am not married and I never eat meat."

In the corner of the room Andrew saw a very, very, very old man. He had no hair, no
teeth and he could not see or hear very well.

"Why do you think you have lived so long, sir?" Andrew asked.

"I smoke forty cigarettes every day, I drink five bottles of wine. I have twenty children.
I only eat meat and chocolate. I never eat fruit."

Andrew was very surprised and said, "And how old are you, sir?"

The man said slowly,

" . . . . "

59   The Polar Bear

Can you guess the last line of this story?

One day a baby polar bear and its mother were standing in the snow at the North Pole. It was snowing and a cold wind was blowing. The baby polar bear looked at its mother and said,

"Mother, am I really a polar bear?"

"Yes, of course you are, son. You are a beautiful polar bear," she said.

After a few seconds the baby polar bear said,

"Are you sure, mother?"

"Of course I'm sure. Look at your fur. Isn't it thick?"

"Yes, mother."

"And your fur is white like the snow, isn't it?"

"Yes, mother."

"And you can swim in the cold sea, can't you?"

"Yes, mother."

"And you can catch fish, can't you?"

"Yes, mother."

"And you have sharp teeth for eating meat, haven't you?"

"Yes, mother."

"And you have hair on your feet to help you walk on ice, haven't you?"

"Yes, mother."

"And all the other animals are frightened of you, aren't they?"

"Yes, mother."

Then the mother polar bear said,

"So, son, I am sure you are a polar bear. Why do you ask?"

The baby polar bear looked up and said,

" . . . . "

Can you guess the last line of this story?

Henry Leech was a salesman. He sold vacuum cleaners. He was a good salesman and he sold lots of vacuum cleaners. One week the manager sent Henry into the countryside. He drove out of town and stopped at a farmhouse. He knocked at the door and the farmer's wife opened it. Henry started talking immediately.

"Madam, how much time do you spend sweeping the floors of this house?"

"A lot of time. This is a farm. The floors get dirty quickly," she replied.

"And how much time do you spend beating the carpets?"

"A lot of time. My husband always forgets to take off his boots."

"And how much time do you spend cleaning the sofa and armchairs?"

"A lot of time. The dog always sits on them," she replied.

Henry smiled at the farmer's wife and said,

"Madam, this is your lucky day. I am going to show you something that will change your life."

Henry showed her his vacuum cleaner and said,

"You can clean the house in minutes with this machine."

The farmer's wife did not look interested.

Henry took out a big bag. It was full of dirt and very small pieces of paper. He opened the bag and threw the dirt and paper over the floor and carpets of the farmhouse. The farmer's wife was very surprised. Before she could speak, Henry said,

"Madam, if this machine does not pick up all the dirt and paper, I will eat the dirt and paper."

The farmer's wife looked at Henry and said,

" . . . . "

Can you guess the last line of this story?

Mr Green opened a grocer's shop when he was twenty years old. For sixty-five years he worked in the shop every day. He worked very hard and he never took a holiday. One day Mr Green was ill. He stayed in bed. The doctor came and examined him. He said to Mr Green's family,

"He is very ill. I'm sorry. There is nothing I can do. He will die soon."

Mr Green's family went into the bedroom after the doctor left. They stood around the bed. Mr Green's eyes were closed. After a few minutes he started to speak in a quiet voice. He said,

"Are you here, Jane?"

"I'm here," said his wife. She was crying softly.

Then Mr Green asked,

"Are you here, Toby?"

"I'm here," said his eldest son. He tried not to cry.

After a few seconds Mr Green said,

"Are you here, Mary ?"

"I'm here, father," said his eldest daughter. She was also crying.

Mr Green asked,

"Are you here, John?"

"I'm here," said the youngest son. He touched his father's hand.

After a minute, Mr Green said,

"Are you here, Lorna?"

"I'm here, father," said the youngest daughter. Her eyes were red.

Suddenly Mr Green opened his eyes. He was very weak but he lifted his head and shouted,

" . . . . "

Can you guess the last line of this story?

A tourist was travelling alone in the desert. After two weeks his car stopped working. He got out and started walking. He was lost and he had no water. It was very hot and he became very thirsty. After five hours he saw a small tent in front of him. There was a woman in the tent. The tourist said to the woman,

"Water. Please sell me some water."

"I'm sorry. I haven't any water. I am taking ties to the market to sell," the woman replied.

The tourist walked on. He became more thirsty. Two kilometres later he came to another small tent. There was an old man in the tent.

"Water. Please sell me some water."

"I'm sorry. I haven't any water. I am taking ties to the market to sell," the man replied.

The tourist put his money back into his pocket and walked on. He was very, very thirsty and also very tired. One kilometre later he arrived at a third tent. There was a man with a beard in the tent. The man said,

"Do you want to buy a tie? I have many beautiful ties."

"No. No. No," shouted the tourist. "I need water. Please sell me water."

"I'm sorry. I only have ties," said the old bearded man.

The tourist fell to the ground and started to crawl. An hour later he saw a large hotel. It was an expensive-looking hotel. The tourist crawled to the door and took out all his money. He said to the doorman,

"Water! I will pay £100 for a glass of water."

The doorman looked at the dirty tourist and said,

"...................................."

63   The Artist

Can you guess the last line of this story?

Charles Dupont was an unknown French artist. He was an extremely talented artist but he painted very slowly. In twenty years Charles had only produced forty paintings. Most people agreed that the quality of his paintings was excellent, but nobody offered Charles much money for them. Charles did not want to sell them cheaply so he kept all of them in his studio.

One day Charles was feeling depressed so he took a long look at his life. After some time he came to the decision that it was time to give up his life as an artist and do something different. He decided to sell all of his paintings.

Charles' father was a baker in a small village. He was getting old and he needed help. As the only child, Charles thought that he would return home and help his father run the bakery. People might not buy his paintings but surely they would buy his bread.

Charles took his forty paintings to a friend who had an art gallery. His friend agreed to help Charles sell his paintings by exhibiting them in the gallery. However, if they had not been sold in three weeks, Charles would have to take them back.

Each day Charles went to the gallery after it closed, but each day he was disappointed. None of his paintings had been sold. On the twenty-first day he met his friend at the gallery door. His friend said, "Do you want the good news or the bad news first?" Charles was excited and asked for the good news.

"Earlier today a man came into the gallery and asked if your paintings would increase in value when you were dead. When I told him that they would probably be worth ten or twenty times as much as they are now, he bought them all."

"Wonderful!" Charles cried in delight. "Now what's the bad news?"

" . . . . "

64   The Businessman

Can you guess the last line of this story?

Mr Kane was a tough but successful businessman. Ten years ago, he started a small business. One day his son, Peter, came to him and said that he wanted to be a businessman like his father. Mr Kane told him that you had to be tough to succeed in business. He wanted Peter to go to university and become a lawyer, a teacher, or a doctor. However, his son was stubborn and refused. He only wanted to be a businessman and urged his father to help him.

"Please, Dad. Teach me how to be a successful businessman."

Reluctantly, Mr Kane agreed to his son's request.

"Okay, Peter. First of all I want you to walk down to the wall at the bottom of the garden." Peter looked at his father and said,

"But what has that got to do with business, dad?"

"Don't ask questions. Trust me and do what I say," he replied. Peter was puzzled but he walked to the wall. His father continued,

"Now climb up the ladder and stand on top of the wall."

Again Peter protested,

"But I don't see how this will help me to be a businessman."

"Don't ask questions. Trust me and do what I say," Mr Kane said.

Peter climbed up the ladder and stood on top of the wall. It was six metres high and Peter felt his legs begin to shake.

"Now. Jump down into the garden," his father said.

"But I can't. I'll injure myself," Peter protested.

"Do you want to become a successful businessman or not?

"Yes, of course," Peter cried.

"Then trust me. I know what I am doing. Jump!"

Peter jumped into the garden and broke both his legs. As he screamed in pain his father came over to him and said,

" . . . . "

65   The Diplomat

Can you guess the last line of this story?

In 1880, there was an important meeting in London to discuss international trade and business between Europe and South East Asia. Over 20 countries sent diplomats to the conference. In the evenings there were formal dinners. The diplomats were often accompanied by their wives or husbands at these functions.

At one dinner, the wife of a British diplomat was placed next to a gentleman from China. Lady Barnes had never seen or met anybody from China before. She felt a little uncomfortable. As she sat down at the table she did not know what to say to him. She wasn't sure if he spoke English so she just smiled. The Chinese gentleman smiled back. They both sat in silence.

Lady Barnes was glad when the soup arrived. It gave her something to talk about. After a few minutes she turned to the Chinese gentleman and in a loud, slow and clear voice she said, "Likee soupee." The Chinese gentleman looked up at her. He smiled and nodded his head. Lady Barnes did not try to begin another conversation and neither did the Chinese gentleman. They completed the meal without speaking another word to each other.

Lady Barnes was very surprised when the Chinese gentleman stood up and began a long speech at the end of the meal. He thanked the British for the wonderful reception they had given the Chinese. He thanked them for their hospitality and for a delicious meal. He said that he was sure that relations between Europe and the Far East would improve because of the meeting of diplomats in London. He spoke perfect English. He was clear, natural and fluent.

When the Chinese gentleman sat down there was great applause from the three hundred guests. He turned to Lady Barnes, who looked very embarrassed, and said,

" . . . . "

66   The Computer

Can you guess the last line of this story?

A group of international scientists decided to design and build the largest and most powerful computer in the world. These scientists believed that such a computer would solve all the complex problems of science and mathematics in seconds.

It took twenty years to build the computer. It was so large that it occupied a building of thirty floors. The scientists were very pleased with their creation. They chose a date on which to introduce the computer to the world and they invited famous scientists to come along and test their computer.

An Italian mathematician had spent five years working on a difficult mathematical problem. When he gave the problem to the computer it answered in two seconds. The Italian mathematician was astounded. "It's correct," he shouted and left the room.

A British scientist had spent his life trying to predict British weather without much success. The ability to predict the weather in Britain is important so that tourists will know the best time to come on holiday. The British scientist gave the computer a lot of facts about the climate in Britain and after ten seconds the computer produced a detailed description for a complete year. The scientist was delighted.

Problem after problem was given to the computer. It solved all of them easily. Soon the eager voices of scientists grew quieter and quieter until there was silence in the room. The scientists had no more questions to ask.

At that moment the lady who was serving tea and coffee shouted to the computer, "Is there a God?" The computer's lights flashed and flashed and flashed. They continued for one minute, then another. The computer had never taken this long to answer. After ten minutes the lights stopped flashing and in a deep voice, the computer replied,

" . . . . "

Can you guess the last line of this story?

Debating is a very popular activity in Great Britain. For the British, it is important to be able to speak well and to speak convincingly. As a result there are many debating clubs and societies in schools and universities to train people to debate well.

Each year there is a competition to find the country's best debater. One year the finalists were Steven Swan from England and Magnus MacDonald from Scotland. They were two very different characters, both in appearance and personality.

Steven Swan was a short and very fat man. He weighed over 200 kilos and he was shaped like a ball. He was a very sociable man. Steven was always with friends and he never stopped talking. He spent a great amount of his time in expensive London restaurants debating with politicians and businessmen. They always paid the bills so Stephen ate enormous amounts of food.

Magnus MacDonald, on the other hand, was almost the complete opposite. He was tall and very, very thin. He looked like a pencil and he seemed to be just skin and bones. Magnus lived in a small Scottish town so he was quite unknown. He was a quiet man who spent most of his time reading books in the library. He never spoke unless it was necessary. 'Never waste words' was one of his favourite sayings.

On the day of the final a large crowd waited anxiously to see and hear the two finalists. They entered the debating room and stood looking at each other. This was the first time that they had met. Magnus was silent. Steven slowly looked at Magnus from head to toe and said,

"So you are Magnus. Looking at you, anybody would think that there was a famine in Scotland."

The crowd laughed. Magnus waited until the laughter had stopped and replied coldly,

" . . . . "

Can you guess the last line of this story?

Mr White was sitting on a train which was travelling from Glasgow to London. The train was quite empty and quiet so Mr White was finding the journey enjoyable and relaxing.

At Birmingham, a man with a long beard got onto the train. He looked a little eccentric. He had pink trousers, a yellow shirt with a green tie, a silver hat, orange socks and bright red shoes.

After a few minutes the man opened a small brown bag and took out some fine white powder. It looked like chalk dust. He started to throw the powder around the railway carriage. He continued doing this for about five minutes. Then he smiled to himself and sat down. Mr White ignored him and kept on reading his newspaper.

However twenty minutes later the man took out his bag again and sprinkled the white powder around the carriage. Mr White continued to ignore the man. However the man kept scattering his powder around the carriage every twenty minutes and this began to irritate Mr White. After two hours Mr White asked angrily,

"Excuse me, but what are you doing?"

The man stopped throwing the white powder and said,

"Look in my bag, sir. This powder is no ordinary powder. This is ANTI-TIGER DUST. It's very special, very rare and very expensive."

In an irritated voice Mr White shouted,

"But why are you throwing it around this railway carriage?"

"Ah," said the man. "By sprinkling it around the carriage I am keeping all the tigers away." Mr White was astonished. How could anybody be so stupid, he thought to himself. He protested to the man,

"But there are no tigers around here!"

The man smiled and said,

" . . . . "

69   The Film Star

B

Can you guess the last line of this story?

Rocky Grant was a very famous and successful film star. He was extremely handsome and an excellent actor. His films were always smash hits and they made lots of money. Rocky's last film 'Rumbol 6' made $250,000,000. As a result of this success, all the big film companies wanted Rocky to work for them, even though Rocky's fees were high. He never worked for less than $10,000,000 a film.

However, there was a small problem. Nobody liked working with Rocky. Film directors found him very difficult. He was so arrogant that he usually tried to tell the directors what to do. The other actors also found him impossible to work with. Rocky always complained that they were amateurs and not good enough to work with him. As a result, very few people talked to him.

Rocky was also very unsociable. He never bought drinks or presents for the people he worked with, and he never invited anybody to his huge luxury home. The only thing that Rocky liked to do was talk about money. He talked about his houses, his private planes, his collection of paintings and other possessions. He always talked about himself. He never asked if you were well or not.

One morning while they were filming a scene for the film 'The Last Millionaire', a young cameraman came up to Rocky. He asked Rocky politely if he would move to the side so that he could get past with his camera. Rocky looked angrily at the young man and started shouting at the top of his voice,

"Do you know who you are talking to? I'm Rocky Grant, the world's most famous film star. I've made over one hundred films. I'm one of the world's richest men. I've got $1,000,000,000 in the bank. Now, young man. What have you got?"

The cameraman listened to Rocky calmly, then said,

" . . . . "

Can you guess the last line of this story?

Matthews and Sons were a firm of lawyers in London. They were a very old and much respected company. They had been established by Benjamin Matthews in 1770. They were also a fairly large company. Sixty lawyers worked there. However, all of these lawyers were men. No woman had ever worked for the company. In today's world this situation was embarrassing.

At a meeting one day, Sir Reginald Matthews, the head of the firm, said that they would have to employ a female lawyer. The lawyers agreed and after a long series of interviews Jenny Thatcher was chosen. Jenny was a hard-working, assertive woman who got things done efficiently and quickly. She soon established a reputation for good service. This pleased Sir Reginald.

As long as anybody could remember, the weekly meetings of the lawyers had been quiet and peaceful. At these meetings important policy decisions were made. However, none of the lawyers had ever dared to question or argue with the decisions taken by Sir Reginald Matthews.

A few months after her arrival at the company Jenny Thatcher began to disagree with some of Sir Reginald's decisions. The situation gradually got worse. After a few months they argued at every meeting. After six months they had stopped talking politely to each other. They simply shouted at each other. Meetings were now battles. At one meeting Sir Reginald got very angry with Jenny when she said that he was not able to run the company. She said that he should retire and hand it over to somebody younger. Sir Reginald looked Jenny in the eye and said,

"Miss Thatcher. You are impossible. If you were my wife I would put poison in your tea."

The men in the room giggled. Jenny looked at Sir Reginald and said,

" . . . . "

71   The Parking Space

Can you guess the last line of this story?

Alan Bell was 18. He drove a Mini, which is a very small British car. Alan loved his car and he washed and polished it every day.

Last weekend he went into the centre of London, where it was busy and very difficult to find a parking space. After thirty minutes Alan found an empty parking space but he did not park his car in the space. Instead, he waited about thirty metres from it. A minute later a car stopped and began to reverse into the space. Alan raced forward in his Mini and sped into the empty parking space ahead of the other car. Alan got out of his car and said,

"You have to be young and very fast to do that."

When the angry driver drove away Alan got back into his car and drove out of the space. Once again he waited about thirty metres from the empty space.

The next car to come along was a beautiful white Rolls-Royce. The driver was an old man. He started to reverse slowly into the parking space. However Alan raced forward and shot into the empty space. Proudly, he got out of his car and looked at the old man who had rolled down the window of his Rolls-Royce. Alan said,

"You have to be young and very fast to do that."

The old man did not look angry and he did not drive away. Instead he reversed his car into the back of Alan's Mini. He went forward and then he reversed into the Mini again. Alan watched in horror as the big car smashed into his little Mini. After a few minutes his car was a wreck. He would not be able to drive it again. Alan stood with his mouth wide-open, staring blankly at the driver of the Rolls Royce.

The old man got out of the Rolls-Royce, which was also badly damaged. He handed Alan a card with his insurance details on it. He smiled and said,

" . . . . "

B

Can you guess the last line of this story?

Christian Gibson was a famous and successful fashion designer. His clothes were sold in the world's most exclusive shops. These clothes weren't cheap. A single dress could cost £5,000. Film stars, kings and queens were his regular customers.

Christian was 54. He was a passionate man but his marriages never seemed to last long. He had been married and divorced five times. He was still friendly with his ex-wives and met them frequently. For Christian, women were the most desirable things in the world and he spent much of his time chasing them.

One July, Christian was at an international fashion show in Singapore. At a formal dinner party one evening, he became quite bored with the people at his table. He lit a cigar and looked round the room at the other tables and the people sitting at them. At one table he gazed in astonishment at the most beautiful woman he had ever seen. The woman was tall, blonde, with a face like an angel. Her eyes sparkled and were as blue as the sea. Her teeth were like snow and her smile warmed his heart. She was amazingly beautiful.

Christian's heart began to beat quickly. He decided that he had to meet this sensual woman. Luckily, he noticed that his second wife was also sitting at the table. She appeared to know the woman. He watched them talking amiably together. Then he took out a small sheet of notepaper and wrote, 'Who is that incredibly beautiful woman at the table?' He folded the paper and handed it to a waiter. He told the waiter to give it discreetly to his ex-wife.

Christian's second wife read the note. She looked at her gorgeous friend and then across at Christian. She smiled and wrote something on the notepaper. She sent the note back to Christian who snatched the note from the waiter. His hands shook as he unfolded it.

The note said,

" . . . . "

Can you guess the last line of this story?

Nigel Cavendish was a very famous British spy. For over twenty years he had successfully stolen important secrets from countries all over the world. Everybody in Great Britain knew his name but very few people knew what he looked like. The newspapers described his daring adventures but they never showed a photograph of him. Nigel was a national hero with no face.

However, in 1917, Nigel's luck finally ran out. He was captured in a foreign country while trying to steal some important military documents. He was taken to court and shown to the world. As a spy there was no mercy, and he was sentenced to death. He was to be executed at dawn by firing squad.

On the day of his execution the weather was terrible. The sky was black. It was raining very heavily and a cold north wind was blowing. At seven o'clock in the morning a group of soldiers arrived at Nigel's prison cell. Nigel stood between the soldiers and they marched him across the prison yard.

They walked for about four hundred metres to a wall. On the way they had to walk through puddles of water and their feet got very wet and muddy. The rain kept pouring down and their clothes were soon soaked. They all felt cold and miserable. When they reached the wall one of the soldiers placed Nigel against it. The soldier tied Nigel's arms behind his back. Before he put a blindfold over his eyes, he asked Nigel if he wished to say anything before he died. Nigel looked up at the black sky and in an angry and bitter voice, he said,

"What horrible men you are – to bring me out to be shot on such a terrible day."

The soldier studied the grey sky above him and replied,

" . . . . "

Can you guess the last line of this story?

Clive Donovan was a sheep farmer in Australia about a hundred years ago. He lived a very solitary life on his sheep farm four hundred kilometres from the nearest town. Clive was not used to company so he did not say much. He was also a strict man who did not like to be disobeyed or criticised.

One day Clive read an article in the newspaper about a small group of young English women who wanted to come to Australia to marry Australian men. Clive wrote to the group and for the next six months he exchanged letters with a young lady called Mary Calderwood. To his surprise, Mary agreed to marry him.

Three months later Clive drove his wagon to the nearest railway station to meet Mary. The wagon was pulled by two horses. Clive helped Mary up onto the wagon and they began the long journey to the farm. Clive did not say a word. Mary thought that living alone for so long had probably made him very shy. She decided to stay quiet.

After a kilometre one of the horses stood on a stone and stumbled. This shook the wagon and made Clive angry. He stood up, pointed at the horse and shouted, "That's one." Clive sat down again and they continued their journey in silence.

Ten kilometres later the same horse stumbled again. Clive pointed a finger at the horse and shouted angrily, "That's two." Mary thought that she saw fear in the eyes of the horse. She was new to Australia so she decided not to ask any questions.

However, twenty kilometres later the unfortunate horse stumbled for the third time. "That's three," thundered Clive as he jumped down from the wagon. He took out his gun and shot the terrified horse between the eyes. Mary was shocked. "Why did you do that?" she protested. "How could you do such a cruel and stupid thing?"

Clive turned slowly to his young wife and said,

" . . . . "

75   The Space Race

Can you guess the last line of this story?

During the 1950's and the 1960's the United States of America and Russia took part in a race to put a man into space. Large amounts of money were spent and some of the most intelligent scientists worked together to design rockets to carry people into space. The Russians were the first country to put a man into space when Yuri Gagarin circled the Earth. The Russians were very proud. They were ahead in the space race. However, the Americans won the next stage in the race. On the 20th of July 1969, Neil Armstrong became the first man to step onto the surface of the Moon. The Americans were proud and they were ahead in the space race.

The British, who had been a strong scientific power in the early part of the 20th century, were jealous. All the best British scientists had gone to work for the Americans because they were paid higher salaries and had better research facilities. The space scientists who remained in Great Britain had very little money to develop a British space programme.

In 1970 there was a big party in New York to celebrate the American landing on the Moon. One of the British scientists sent to the party decided to make a speech. He said proudly,

"We are planning to land a man on the Sun. The Russians were first into space. The Americans were the first to the Moon. However, the British will be the first to the Sun."

An astonished Russian scientist asked,

"What will you do about the intense heat and light? Have you developed new materials that won't be melted by the sun?"

An American scientist added,

"What about the sun's radiation? How will you protect the astronauts against it?"

The British scientist laughed and said,

" . . . . "

Can you guess the last line of this story?

Long ago in Greece the people of Sparta were very strong. Spartan soldiers were well-trained. They were skilful in battle and they fought like lions. They were so brave that they would die rather than accept defeat. Every Greek respected them.

The people of Athens were more artistic and cultured. However, in time, the city became bigger and more powerful. One year the leaders of the city decided to send an army to Sparta to attack and defeat the Spartans.

As the army approached Sparta, a single Spartan soldier appeared. He pointed at the Athenian soldiers and said,

"You should go home and talk philosophy. You might get hurt here."

The Athenian general laughed and ordered ten of his men to kill the Spartan. The soldiers ran after the Spartan who disappeared behind a small hill. There was a lot of noise and shouting, then the Spartan appeared again and pointed at the general,

"I'm warning you. You should go home or you will all get hurt."

The Athenian general was angry. He ordered two hundred of his men to kill the Spartan. Again the soldiers chased the Spartan behind the hill. There was the sound of shouting and screaming. After fifteen minutes the noise stopped and there was silence. The general and his soldiers waited anxiously. Then the Spartan walked out from behind the hill and said,

"I warned you. Now I'm angry so you are all going to die."

The Athenian general was absolutely furious. He turned to his soldiers and ordered all of them to attack the Spartan. As the three thousand soldiers started to run forward, a single Athenian soldier crawled over the hill behind the Spartan. He was very weak and he had blood on his face. He lifted his arm and shouted,

" .... "

Can you guess the last line of this story?

John was a very intelligent young boy. His parents were ordinary people who did not have much money, but John won a scholarship to a very famous private school. Most of the other boys came from very rich families. John's parents had left school when they were very young so they were not very well-educated.

Quite often John came home from school and used long words that his mother and father did not understand. One day he returned from school and said to his mother,

"Mum, may I relate to you a narrative?"

"What is a narrative?" she asked.

"A narrative is a tale, a kind of story, mother."

"Oh, I see," said the mother.

So John told her a long tale about a king who wanted to be a bird. It was such a long story that it was time to go to bed when he finished. As John was leaving the room he said to his mother,

"Shall I extinguish the light?"

"What does 'extinguish' mean?"his mother asked.

"To 'extinguish something' means to 'put something out'," said John.

"Oh, I see," said his mother. "Yes. Put the light out."

The next day John's mother was very nervous. The headmaster was coming to have tea at their house to talk about John's excellent progress. John's mother wanted to sound like an educated woman.

The headmaster arrived. John's mother gave him a cup of tea and one of her home-made pies which she had spent all morning baking. The pies were just out of the oven and they smelled delicious. John, his mother, and the headmaster sat down together. While they were eating, the family dog became excited by the smell of the pies. It began to bark and jump up and down. John's mother wanted to impress the headmaster so she said to John,

" . . . . "

78   Business Ethics

Can you guess the last line of this story?

Shrewd & Thrifty were a small but relatively successful retailer of electrical goods. The company had been founded by Edgar Shrewd and Timothy Thrifty. Both men worked hard and both displayed a high degree of business acumen. Year after year they impressed rival companies with the healthy profit margins they achieved, and they surprised some of the large national retailers by maintaining these margins in times of economic recession. These performances had led to a number of takeover bids from the large retailers but both partners always stood firm and adamantly refused to sell out. They were committed to the idea of a family business and they expected their sons and daughters to follow in their footsteps into the family firm.

Steven Shrewd had just turned sixteen and rejoiced in the fact that he could leave school. Every subject was boring, tedious and unexciting, except for Mathematics. Steven could spend hours totting up figures and never tired of it.

For as long as he could remember, all he had ever wanted to do was to work in his father's store. He dreamt of turning Shrewd & Thrifty into a multi-national conglomerate with stores spanning the globe. Steven became a trainee manager with the company. He shadowed his father to pick up all there was to know about running the company. Apart from the practical side of the business, Steven spent a lot of time reading up on all aspects of business matters. However this was not an activity he had much stamina for. He usually approached his father for explanations of crucial business terminology or notions. One day he asked his father,

"Dad. What do they mean when they write about 'business ethics'?"

Mr Shrewd reflected deeply for a few moments. Then he replied,

"Son. This is probably one of the most difficult areas of business to understand, master and practise. Business ethics raises some of the most demanding questions and dilemmas for the businessman to answer."

"What kind of questions are they?" asked Steven eagerly.

"Perhaps the best way for me to explain this to you is through a concrete example. Suppose a customer comes into the store and buys a small appliance which costs £5. The customer gives you a £20 note which you ring up on the till. However, when you turn round, you find that the customer has already left, forgetting about the £15 change which you have in your hand. Have you got the picture, son?"

"Sure, Dad."

"Now. Here is where a question of business ethics arises," Mr Shrewd said with a gleam in his eye.

"What is it, Dad?" Steven asked with great anticipation.

His father said slowly and with excessive stress,

" . . . . "

79   The Butcher's Dance

Can you guess the last line of this story?

There are substantial tracts of the dense tropical rainforests of Borneo in South-East Asia that remain relatively unexplored by man. Common to many of the small tribes that inhabit these areas are the rituals of head-hunting and head-shrinking, activities which send shivers down the spines of those in the so-called civilised countries.

In the early 1950's a German expert in cannibalism made contact with a tribe called the Makanorang. Unfortunately, all that is known of this contact was gleaned from the scant notes of a weather-beaten diary found next to a skeleton by a group of British anthropologists. It was impossible to tell from the remains of the German anthropologist if he had died violently or from some tropical disease.

The diary crumbled as it was opened. However, a crude map indicated the location of the Makanorang and from the notes it seemed that the German had become convinced that the tribe had been visited by British colonialists in the 1930's. The British anthropologists were curious as there was nothing in their records about this meeting. The last entry in the diary read, 'Today is the Butcher's Dance'. Curiously the German had written the name of the dance in English, the only two words of English in the diary. This fact baffled the British. The anthropologists debated whether to return home or not, but in the end they judged themselves to be sufficiently numerous and well-armed to press on and solve the enigma of the 'Butcher's Dance'.

Two weeks later the nervous anthropologists were given a friendly welcome by the Makanorang. Accommodation was provided. Food was copious. No aggression was displayed and there appeared to be a complete absence of weapons. The Makanorang did not seem to be hunters, subsisting almost entirely on fruit and berries. Most of the day was spent having fun, with adults and children playing a variety of simple games. About two months later the anthropologists learned that at the next full moon, the Butcher's Dance would take place.

A week before this event the mood of the village changed dramatically. The anthropologists were ignored and the villagers became more and more introverted, spending hours and hours painting themselves. On the day of the dance the Makanorang spent the morning getting drunk on a fermented fruit drink. At noon as their behaviour became more and more frantic, they disappeared into the jungle.

As dusk fell and the full moon began to rise above the horizon, the headman reappeared and beckoned the edgy anthropologists to a raised platform in the centre of the village. As they sat down, drums began to beat from the surrounding jungle. Then the Makanorang emerged from the edges of the jungle carrying long pointed sticks. The anthropologists fingered the revolvers in their pockets nervously. The Makanorang slowly encircled them, then stopped abruptly. The headman looked at the trembling anthropologists and smiled. Then he raised his hand and shouted,

" . . . . "

Can you guess the last line of this story?

A faux pas is when someone does something to create a socially embarrassing situation through words or behaviour. For example, if at a party I innocently offered an alcoholic drink to a Muslim, or pork to a Jew, this would be considered a faux pas, a gaffe, a blunder, or more idiomatically, you would say that 'I had dropped a brick.' Most of us have dropped bricks at some time in our lives.

The well-known British conductor Malcolm Sargent once took his leading soloist to the Royal Box during the interval of a concert and said,

"Your Majesty, may I introduce Sergio Poliakoff? Sergio, meet the King of Norway."

The distinguished figure shifted uncomfortably, then said "Sweden".

The world-famous American conductor, André Previn, recalls one horrendous faux pas he made while he was the resident conductor of the London Symphony Orchestra. It was André's custom to unwind and relax in the bar of a nearby hotel after rehearsals and performances. He often spent his time talking to guest musicians. The bar was also a perfect setting for aspiring young musicians and composers to seek him out to make themselves known and perhaps get that lucky break which would propel them into the limelight.

One evening André was sitting in the bar of the Westbury Hotel when he recognised a young American composer coming into the hotel. The American looked a little lost as his eyes searched the room for a friendly face. André raised a hand and beckoned him over. He invited him to join him for a drink and conversation turned inevitably to music and to the young composer's work which André very much admired.

The young composer made polite enquiries about the forthcoming concert by the London Symphony Orchestra. Wishing to be complimentary to his host, he said,

"I heard your orchestra a few nights ago. It sounded absolutely marvellous."

"Exactly which night was that?" inquired André.

"It was the night that Beethoven's Sixth was played in the first half."

André thanked the young composer for his gracious comments but then he had a sudden recollection of that night.

"Oh God," André groaned. "That was the night Pollini was supposed to play the Fourth Piano Concerto in the second half. Unfortunately he cancelled at short notice and we were stuck with one of those last-minute substitutions. She turned out to be a really appalling, third-rate pianist. I'm really sorry you had to suffer through that."

The young composer was silent for a few moments. He gave André a long and thoughtful look. Then he said,

" . . . . "

81 Fate

C

Can you guess the last line of this story?

Harry had been a promising footballer. Born in Wales in 1966, the year the English national football team won the World Cup, he had devoted his life to football. Years of practice paid off and at fifteen he became the youngest member of a first division team. At sixteen he won his first cap when he represented Wales in an international against their arch-rivals England. Unfortunately, his debut was marred by a heavy defeat. At twenty, he fulfilled one of his dreams when he became captain of the Welsh team. His sole remaining ambition was to see Wales win the World Cup.

Three months before the 1986 World Cup Finals in Mexico, disaster struck. During a league match, Harry was badly tackled by the English international, Peter Butcher. Butcher was sent off immediately while Harry was rushed to hospital writhing in pain. Four hours later, a grim-faced doctor informed Harry that he would never play professional football again. His leg had suffered multiple fractures around the ankle and his knee had been so badly twisted that many of the main ligaments had been torn beyond repair. Harry was devastated. However, he agreed to accompany the Welsh team to Mexico City for the World Cup Finals as their coach – the next best thing to playing.

One night Harry fell into conversation with the physiotherapist of the Mexican national team and told him about his leg and how his career had been cruelly cut short. Deep down Harry believed that there had to be some cure or treatment somewhere in the world for his leg. The Mexican physiotherapist examined Harry's leg but he too considered the damage irreversible. However, he had heard of a witch doctor who lived in the north of the country who claimed to be able to alter fate. Although this sounded preposterous, Harry was willing to try anything.

Harry travelled high into the mountains and after a gruelling trek over rough and dangerous paths he came to a cave. He entered and when his eyes grew accustomed to the dark he made out the seated figure of the witch doctor. He sat down beside him. The witch doctor began to eat peyote leaves and his eyes grew brighter and brighter. Suddenly he fell into a trance and a deep voice said,

"How can I help you?"

Harry talked about his leg and with tears running down his cheeks he pleaded,

"Can you alter my fate so that my leg is not damaged?"

After a ponderous silence, the witch doctor's weary voice continued,

"To alter fate is difficult. Although events are already determined, although each man's fate is predestined, it is much easier to change future events than past events. I do not think I have sufficient power to enter the past and restore your leg."

"Well, as a compensation," Harry continued, "Could you arrange things so that Wales meet England in the World Cup Final in six weeks' time and thrash them?"

The witch doctor stared into space and then said,

"   . . . .   "

Ⓒ

Can you guess the last line of this story?

Many of the most respected and influential members of society belong to golf clubs and use golf as a means of socialising and relaxation. Paradoxically, the game can be a constant source of frustration as the results players achieve inevitably fall short of their expectations. As such, it is not uncommon for the air to turn blue on the golf course, and temper tantrums are by no means unknown.

One day Harold Runcie, the vicar of Melford, was playing golf with Winston Sharp, a prominent brain surgeon. They were a good match for each other and enjoyed the close competitions that they usually had. A small wager of £10 had been placed on the outcome of the game.

After fifteen holes and with only three holes remaining, the match was level. At the sixteenth hole, with his ball only one metre from the hole, Winston had one shot to win the hole. Winston's work involved him in making some of the most delicate and accurate muscular movements that the human hand is capable of. Daily he carried out life-saving operations on the human brain, where one small slip of the scalpel could cause death or permanent brain damage. Yet the same man on the golf course facing a task which demands far less muscular co-ordination and accuracy somehow begins to doubt whether he can put the ball in the hole. Winston hit his ball and it slid past the hole. His anger was immediate,

"God! Missed! How could I miss from such a distance?"

"Now, Winston," said the vicar. " Control yourself. You mustn't take the Lord's name in vain. You may incur his wrath."

Winston said nothing. He seethed with anger. At the next hole Winston faced a similar shot to win. This time his ball was only half a metre from the hole. Once again doubt intervened and he missed.

"Good God! Missed again. This is impossible. Harold, have you got your Boss working for you?"

"Control yourself, Winston. It is only a game. And please don't take the Lord's name in vain. He may strike you down in anger."

At the final hole Winston had an extremely short shot of about twenty centimetres to win the hole and the match. However he failed to hit the ball hard enough. It teetered on the edge of the hole but refused to drop. Winston couldn't control himself.

"God! God! God! . . . ."

His outburst was interrupted by an enormous bolt of lightning which ripped through the air towards the two golfers. There was a huge explosion and smoke filled the air. When the smoke cleared Winston was standing in a daze but there was a deep crater where the vicar had been standing. As the deafening clap of thunder that followed the lightning faded away, a deep authoritative voice from the heavens said,

" . . . . "

83   Happiness

Can you guess the last line of this story?

This story is set at a time when the KGB, the Russian secret police, were a much feared force in the USSR. Soviet citizens lived in fear of being denounced, arrested in the early hours of the morning, and sent to labour camps.

The story takes place in a restaurant in New York where a British diplomat, a French diplomat and a Russian diplomat are having an informal meal following a United Nations conference on nuclear disarmament. The wine and food had been excellent and conversation turned away from the complexities of world politics to the simple pleasures of life, and the need to be happy. A philosophical waiter, passing their table, asked "But what is happiness, gentlemen?"

The French diplomat was first to respond. Waving his hands excitedly, he said, "For me, happiness is sitting in a café on the banks of the River Seine in Paris in late spring, watching the sun sink slowly over the city's magnificent cathedrals, buildings and bridges. It is to sit there and leisurely sip the fine wines of the Rhone valley and savour the rich variety of French cheeses."

The British diplomat followed.

"For me, happiness is found in the home. As the old saying goes, 'An Englishman's home is his castle.' Happiness is to sit in the study, in front of a roaring wood fire, with a glass of the finest Scotch malt whisky in my hand, looking out across lush, green fields at the cattle and the sheep peacefully grazing."

Satisfied with themselves and the images they had evoked, the French and the British diplomats looked expectantly towards the Russian diplomat.

"For me, happiness is to be in my tiny two-bedroomed flat in the centre of Moscow, listening to the neighbours arguing through the paper thin walls. It is to sit in this damp, crowded room around a small inefficient heater with my wife and six screaming children, drinking cheap vodka while watching the cockroaches scuttle across the floor."

The British and French diplomats raised their eyebrows in disbelief.

"And then," the Russian continued, "there is a knock at the door at five o'clock in the morning. I stare through the keyhole and see a KGB colonel and two uniformed soldiers with machine-guns. I rush to the bedroom and wake up my wife and children. Then with tears streaming down my face I embrace them all tightly for the last time, falsely assuring them that I will be back soon. I open the door and the harsh voice of the colonel rasps,

"Petrov. You are under arrest."

As the Russian paused, the French diplomat asked incredulously,

"But surely, this is a perverse sense of happiness?"

The Russian continued,

"

"

. . . .

Can you guess the last line of this story?

In the 1960's, large packs of youths on motorcycles were a common sight on the open highways of the United States of America. These groups were uniform in appearance, easily recognised by their long hair and black leather jackets. They had a very bad reputation for aggressive and destructive behaviour. Most considered themselves rebels and had little respect for law and order. They were called Hell's Angels and individual packs were known as chapters.

One hot summer, a chapter of about thirty Hell's Angels from San Francisco were cruising along an empty Californian highway looking for fun, which was generally at the expense of the general public. The first hour was spent encircling cars with their bikes and glaring with malice through the windows. This was guaranteed to put the fear of death into the occupants who had been fed by the media with unsubstantiated stories of robbery, rape and murder. The Angels thrived on such infamy.

Around noon and tiring of the game they came across a small roadside restaurant. The leader of the chapter led the pack into the relatively empty parking area and informed the others that it was time to have some more 'fun'. With broad grins on their faces, the group entered the café which was almost deserted. The owner was cleaning some glasses behind the counter, while two rather ordinary-looking men sat quietly at the back of the café. They were absorbed in their meals and newspapers. As the door was slammed shut, the largest of the men threw his newspaper into the air, leaped to his feet and rushed out of the back door with a terrified look on his face. The Angels laughed derisively.

Three Angels strode nonchalantly across to the remaining diner, who was short, skinny and balding. They surrounded his small table and stared menacingly at him. He seemed oblivious to their presence. One of the Angels took the buttered roll out of the man's hand and began to stuff it into his own mouth. The man failed to react. A second Angel tore the newspaper from the man's hands and slowly ripped it to shreds. The man made no eye contact with the Angels. Then the leader took the fried egg from the man's breakfast plate and placed it neatly on top of the man's head, completely covering the bald area. This comic sight was greeted with uproarious laughter and stamping of feet.

Despite this provocation and humiliation the man continued to sit with a stony face. Then, as the fried egg slid from his head, he rose to his feet slowly, and with head bowed submissively, he left the café without saying a word. With a smirk on his face the leader watched the man leave. Then he strolled to the counter and said disparagingly to the owner,

"Not much of a man, eh?"

The owner reflected for a moment and replied,

" .... "

85   The Lion's Share

Can you guess the last line of this story?

The lion is the 'king' of all animals. It is majestic, powerful – an animal to be feared and respected. The fox does not have the strength of the lion but it compensates for its lack of physical prowess with its clever thinking. Apart from the human animal it is generally recognised and respected as the most cunning of creatures. The vulture, on the other hand, suffers the misfortune of being associated with only negative qualities. This is a tale that involves these three creatures.

One day a lion, a fox, and a vulture met by a water hole. They were starving. There was a drought in the region as the rains had not materialised. Food was scarce because many of the animals which the carnivores preyed upon had migrated south in search of somewhere new to graze.

The lion, the fox, and the vulture grumbled about the amount of time they had to spend hunting and how often such hunts were fruitless. Then the fox had an idea.

"Why don't we form a company? Why don't we pool our resources?"

"Come again?" said the vulture.

"Put simply, we work together. We cooperate. I will use my cunning to lure the prey into a trap. Lion will use his speed, claws and teeth to kill the prey and you, vulture, will transport the kill to the water hole where we can feast upon it later."

"Wonderful," cried the vulture. "Can we count you in, Lion?"

The lion nodded. There was a brief shaking of paws and wings, then the hunting party set out. The collaboration proved extremely successful and the kill was good. The vulture had to carry thirty carcasses of various sizes back to the water hole.

As the sun began to set, the three ravenous animals gathered at the water hole. They licked their lips and prepared to gorge themselves. The lion said,

"Partner Vulture. Divide the kill into three equal parts. Then we can eat."

The vulture leapt to his task with enthusiasm and in no time at all he had produced three piles of equal size. The vulture stood proudly by his work but his expression of satisfaction turned to horror when the lion sprang towards him and killed him with one mighty blow of its paw. The lion picked up the limp body of the vulture and threw it onto one of the three piles. It turned to the fox,

"Partner Fox. Divide the kill into two equal parts. Then we can begin to eat."

The fox pushed all the carcasses together into one pile. Then it extracted the body of the smallest animal from the enormous mound of food and placed it to the side. The fox pointed to the large heap of food and said in a servile voice,

"Partner Lion. This heap is your half and the dead rabbit will be my half."

The lion roared with laughter and said,

"Excellent, Fox. Tell me. Who taught you to divide so cleverly into equal halves?"

The fox looked up and smiled,

"..."

Can you guess the last line of this story?

Jock McPherson was careful with his money, never buying on impulse and always demanding good value for his hard-earned cash. Jock was an itinerant worker, employed in the building trade and constantly moving round the country from one building-site to another. One year he took up work on a site in London.

Jock took great care in choosing a boarding house. He eventually found one to his satisfaction, run by a Mrs Pride, who took great pride in the quality of service she provided. Her rooms were spotless, the service prompt and friendly, and her substantial breakfasts had become a legend. In thirty years of business she had never encountered a single dissatisfied customer.

Mrs Pride usually provided only bed and breakfast but Jock, through gentle persuasion rather than charm, made an arrangement with her to provide him with lunch each working day. Jock and Mrs Pride eventually settled on a price for this extra service. However Mrs Pride was somewhat taken aback when Jock produced a large container for his lunch. It looked more like a suitcase than a lunchbox.

On the first morning Mrs Pride made up a large sandwich. She placed her best cold meats on the the sandwich and filled it with generous amounts of salad. The sandwich was substantial enough to provide a meal for two men. When Jock returned from work Mrs Pride asked him eagerly about his lunch.

"Pretty good," Jock said. Then he added, "What there was of it."

Mrs Pride was hurt but she hid her disappointment.

The next morning she prepared two sandwiches, each one bigger that the one she had given to Jock on the first morning. She bought the best cheeses and cold meats and placed alternate layers of cheese, salad and meat on them. They were so thick that she wondered if Jock would be able to get his mouth round them. However she had a point to make and surely he couldn't complain this time. That evening Mrs Pride asked Jock how he had found lunch.

"Pretty good," he said without a smile. Then he added, "What there was of it."

Mrs Pride was outraged but she kept it to herself, giving no overt indication of the hurt and anger that coursed through her. She was determined at all costs to maintain her reputation of always satisfying her customers.

That night she went to her local baker and asked him to bake her a special loaf of bread, one metre square. This would completely fill Jock's lunchbox. Mrs Pride sliced the loaf down the middle and stuffed it full of cheeses, meats, salads, fish and relishes. The sandwich was so bulky and heavy that she needed assistance in lifting it into the lunchbox.

The following day Mrs Pride waited eagerly for Jock to return. When he came into the boarding house he did not wait for Mrs Pride to question him. He said,

"   "

Can you guess the last line of this story?

David Bruce, better known as 'Wee Davy', had one trait which irritated his friends. No matter who they were talking about, David always said he knew them. In fact, he seemed to know almost anybody of importance. Most of the time David's friends humoured him but to no avail. As the years passed David's claims became more and more extravagant.

One night David and a group of his friends were in a pub discussing the forthcoming tour of the rock star Madonna. Sure enough David said he knew her. The friends secretly bought David a ticket and dragged him reluctantly along to the concert. About half way through her show Madonna leapt off the stage into the audience. She rushed up to David and hugged him. Together they returned to the stage. Madonna announced to the audience,

"I would like to introduce a very dear friend of mine to you. Wee Davy."

The friends were astonished but some thought the meeting had been orchestrated. When talk turned to the British Royal Family, David said that he knew all of them. A few weeks later Queen Elizabeth was to open a new hospital in the local area. David was egged on by his friends to go along and prove that he was at least an acquaintance of the Queen. So they stood at the side of the road as the royal procession made its way to the hospital. As the Rolls-Royce came abreast of David's group it stopped abruptly and the Queen emerged with a broad smile on her face and her hand extended in David's direction.

"Wee Davy. How nice to see you again. You must drop into the palace for tea next time you are in London."

David's friends were flabbergasted but some remained sceptical.

One day conversation turned to religion and David mentioned that he was a good friend of the Pope. Nobody could remember David travelling outside the United Kingdom and found this claim difficult to believe. A few of his richer friends decided to call his bluff once and for all. They bought tickets to Rome and insisted that they all visit the Vatican. Somewhat reluctantly, David agreed.

When they arrived at the Vatican they were told that they could not gain admittance to the Pope's private quarters. David went up to the guard and whispered in his ear. He returned to his friends and said that he would be allowed inside and he would bring the Pope out onto the balcony overlooking St Peter's Square.

An hour later, two figures appeared on the balcony. However, the distance made it difficult to make out who they were, although one was clearly dressed in white robes. One of David's friends turned to a passing Italian and said,

"Excuse me. Could you tell me who the man up there in white is?"

The Italian looked up and replied promptly,

" . . . . "

88   The Misogynist

Can you guess the last line of this story?

General Gruff had devoted his entire life to the army. On the basis of a number of brilliantly fought battles he had become a household name in Great Britain and his company was much sought after. However the general found the social situations into which his fame projected him tiresome and intolerable. He was contemptuous of all other occupations, especially those connected with diplomacy.

At formal dinners and functions in which he sat side by side with ambassadors and diplomats he had earned a reputation for having a sharp tongue. Rumour had it that he was also a misogynist. He tended to spend as little time as possible in the company of women. His reason for remaining a bachelor was his belief that all women were obsessed with appearance and the subject of ageing. Both topics were anathema to him. Over the years he had developed a simple but effective strategy of curtailing conversations with women through deliberate rudeness.

On one occasion at a dinner party he had been seated beside the wife of a high-ranking American diplomat who, proud of her youthful appearance and particularly fond of flirtatious behaviour, said, "I'm forty-four but I don't look it, do I?"

"No, but you used to," replied the general drily.

On another occasion an English duchess who was one of the General's many admirers said to him as he was leaving one of her soirées,

"I hope you will come to my parties when I am old and ugly, General?"

"I do," said the general coldly, as he swept out of the door.

In the 1920's, the General was engaged in a campaign in the Middle East. It was late summer and extremely hot. When the General was summoned to a British Embassy garden party in Cairo to honour the visit of a famous British actress, he fumed and boiled with rage. At the party, he stood angrily but quietly in the background. He sipped his drink and glanced frequently at his watch. He was determined to get back to his war at the first possible opportunity. He exchanged a few perfunctory remarks with officials he knew. From a distance he watched the middle-aged actress, heavily made-up, making her way around the guests. The general detested the arts and scowled when he considered the attention being paid to this woman.

The actress had heard a lot about the General and had been drawn to the strong sense of masculinity that his exploits and appearance seemed to convey. She eventually spotted him in the corner and made straight for him. She had not been officially introduced to the General so she decided to use the hot weather as an excuse for opening a conversation. It was 92 degrees Fahrenheit. She approached him, waving her fan vigorously, and said effusively.

"92 today, General Gruff. Imagine that 92, today!"

The general affected a thin smile and said,

"   . . . .   "

Can you guess the last line of this story?

In deepest Africa, at the height of the colonisation of its many tribes by European countries, a British administrator was sent to a remote village to inform its inhabitants of their new status. He spoke directly to the gathered villagers.

"I am a humble representative of the British government and a proud servant of Queen Victoria. I have come to tell you of the great changes that will take place in your country under British rule. These changes will improve your lives beyond your wildest dreams."

The colonial administrator paused while his message was translated. In response the villagers rose to their feet in unison, struck the air with their fists and shouted 'Pa-tun-ga'. The administrator had expected to find a passive, resigned and subdued people. This apparent display of enthusiasm was a pleasant surprise and he warmed to his task.

"We will build factories, establish banks and businesses. We will create roads and railways to service both the needs of industry and commerce. Your nation will become richer and your standard of living will rise accordingly. All this I promise you in the name of our great Queen Victoria."

Translation once again elicited a mighty cry of 'Pa-tun-ga' from the crowd.

"We will build hospitals and bring you modern health care. Our physicians and their modern medicines will eradicate malaria and most of the debilitating diseases that are endemic in this region. We will make you a strong, healthy body of people."

The cries of 'Pa-tun-ga' grew in intensity.

"We will build you schools and bring the finest teachers to educate you and your children. Within a decade the whole nation will be literate and numerate. We will drag you out of the Middle Ages and into the nineteenth century. Education is the key to progress and British rule will ensure this. Long live Queen Victoria."

"Pa-tun-ga! Pa-tun-ga! Pa-tun-ga!" The villagers were now leaping up and down. The colonial administrator was beginning to get carried away with himself and his oratory grew in pathos and grandeur.

"And British justice. Who has not heard of British justice? We have developed the finest legal system the world has ever known. Crime will disappear from your lands and tribal disputes will be settled without the spilling of blood. British justice ensures a civilised society and that is what you deserve. God save Queen Victoria!"

The cries of 'Pa-tun-ga' echoed round the village square. Feeling pleased with himself the colonial administrator turned to the translator and said,

"Well, that went down very well. And I like the sound of this expression 'Pa-tun-ga'. What exactly does it mean?"

The translator pointed in the direction of the next village and said,

" . . . . "

90   The Rivals

Can you guess the last line of this story?

The two biggest cities in Scotland, Edinburgh and Glasgow, have been rivals for many years. The citizens of Edinburgh consider their city to be one of beauty and culture. They look upon Glasgow as a large, bleak industrial town lacking in both character and history. Of course, the citizens of Glasgow do not agree with this view. They cite their universities, their art galleries and their theatres as obvious examples of education and culture, while they criticise the people of Edinburgh for being snobbish, and lacking in both character and a sense of humour.

One year Edinburgh and Glasgow were both bidding to hold an important conference on European economic policy. Representatives from both cities were sent to Brussels to state their case at an open meeting. Members of the press were among those present and both groups recognised the need to cultivate public support.

One representative of the Edinburgh delegation attempted to influence the awarding committee, and appeal to the press at the same time, by focussing on the human aspects of Edinburgh rather than on the merits of the city's conference and communication facilities. He said,

"I could talk about the beauty of Edinburgh. I could mention its magnificent castle which is recognised as one of the world's finest. I could mention the Edinburgh International Festival which continues to attract ever-increasing numbers of actors, artists and tourists from all corners of the globe. I could mention the fact that the British Queen resides in Edinburgh rather than Glasgow when she comes to Scotland. I could focus on all these things but I won't. Instead I will sum up the suitability of Edinburgh for this conference through a simple story. It is a story of an Edinburgh bank manager who was horrified to receive notification of transfer to a larger branch in Glasgow. Although this was promotion he knew his family would find the move to Glasgow distressing. With a heavy heart he went home and broke the news to his family. His wife bore the news well but his twelve-year-old son could not contain himself. He lifted his eyes and his arms to the sky and exclaimed,

"GOOD-BYE, GOD. WE'RE GOING TO GLASGOW."

There was some minor chuckling in the room as the delegate from Edinburgh resumed his seat, looking rather smug and pleased with himself. Almost immediately a delegate from Glasgow got up and went to the podium. He looked calmly and slowly round the room and then said,

"The delegate from Edinburgh tells the story well and with surprising accuracy. He must be congratulated for doing so, as attention to detail is not generally considered to be one of Edinburgh citizens' strongest qualities. However in recounting what the son of the banker said, a minor inaccuracy has appeared which needs correction. What the boy actually said was,

"   "
. . . .

Can you guess the last line of this story?

A psychologist and a sociologist from Liverpool University in England decided to undertake some research into the possible adverse effects of assembly line work on the sex lives of car workers at the nearby Ford car production plant. The assembly line was shut down and one thousand sexually active men were called to a large hall where they sat down in rows.

The psychologist and the sociologist stood on a raised platform in front of the bemused workforce. The sociologist began to explain the purpose of the survey. The mere suggestion that their sex drive may be diminished by their working conditions was met with a loud outburst of guffawing and stamping of feet as the workers looked incredulously around the hall at each other. The psychologist began the survey.

"Gentlemen. I would like you all to stand."

There was a loud scraping of chairs as the men got to their feet.

"Please sit down if you make love at least once a night."

There was an almighty crash as approximately four hundred men sat down, holding their heads up high. The sociologist noted the numbers, the psychologist continued.

"Sit down if you make love at least once a week."

In response, there was an even greater crash as five hundred men resumed their seats. Of the one hundred men remaining on their feet, one man stood out. He had the broadest smile that the scientists had ever seen. The psychologist continued,

"Once a fortnight."

Ninety-eight relieved men sat down, their ordeal over. The man with the smile remained and it was obvious that the other man was near retirement. His shoulders were stooped and he clutched onto his walking stick to steady himself.

"Once a month," the psychologist continued.

The old man sat down to resounding cheers. The man with the smile simply beamed. He showed no signs of discomfort, shame or embarrassment. The other men whispered to each other and the hall was filled with the sound of giggling.

"Once every two months? . . . Once every three months? . . . Once every four months? . . . Once every five months? . . . Once every six months?"

The man continued to stand and smile broadly. The psychologist continued.

"Once every nine months? . . . . Once a YEAR?"

The man sat down to a stunned silence. The psychologist failed to understand how someone denied one of the basic pleasures of life for the greater part of the year could support such a look of contentment. His curiosity finally got the better of him and he asked the question that was on the lips of everybody in the hall.

"Why are you smiling when you only make love once a year?"

Without the slightest hesitation, the man replied,

" . . . . "

Can you guess the last line of this story?

The Ministry of Health in Great Britain was much disturbed by a series of reports which indicated that the health of the nation was deteriorating. The statistics from a small village just to the north of Glasgow in Scotland, whose inhabitants had the shortest life expectancy in Europe, were particularly worrying.

The Minister of Health introduced a hard-hitting approach to the problem, dispensing with the softly-softly approach that had been relatively ineffectual in previous national health campaigns. He sent medical specialists round the schools and public halls of the country to talk to the people directly. The village to the north of Glasgow was seen as the most appropriate place to launch the campaign.

On the day of the meeting the village hall was packed. The men seemed to be in a celebratory mood and passed bottles of whisky to each other. The children stuffed their faces with chocolate and cakes. It was difficult to see the platform clearly as the air was thick with tobacco smoke. Dr. Feelgood, the country's leading medical expert, entered and screwed up his face as the acrid fumes reached his nostrils.

On a large screen above the platform he projected a photograph of a group of healthy-looking Japanese fishermen and added that they subsisted on a staple diet of fish and vegetables. He then showed a photograph of a group of very obese and unhealthy-looking Japanese and explained that these Japanese had adopted western diets and consumed a lot of cakes and chocolate. Dr. Feelgood said rhetorically,

"And what does this prove to us, ladies and gentlemen?"

After a few seconds of silence he added,

"If you eat a lot of sugar, your health will suffer."

Dr. Feelgood turned to smoking. For dramatic effect he took out a glass container with a pink organ preserved in formaldehyde and placed it in front of him.

"This is a human lung. It is the lung of a non-smoker."

He then took out another glass container with a blackened object inside.

"This is the lung of a smoker, reduced in size, coated with tar, and riddled with cancer. The owner died at thirty-five."

"And what does this prove to us, ladies and gentlemen?"

After a few seconds of silence he added,

"If you smoke, your life will be shorter."

Dr. Feelgood then turned to drink and alcoholic abuse. He filled a large glass with whisky. He produced a large earthworm from his pocket and dropped it into the whisky. The worm wriggled about for a few minutes then fell to the bottom of the glass and lay still. Dr. Feelgood said rhetorically,

"And what does this prove to us, ladies and gentlemen?"

Before he could continue a voice from the back of the hall said,

" . . . . "

Answer Key

Section 1

1. 1E 2A 3C 4F 5I 6D 7G 8B 9H
2. 1. drop 2. see 3. fall 4. let 5. pick 6. step 7. drive 8. put 9. hold
3. 1. hopping 2. light 3. lame 4. clean 5. splitting 6. smashing 7. grave 8. sweet 9. Filthy
4. 1. change 2. pretty ugly 3. poor 4. fork 5. present 6. atmosphere 7. charge 8. Fine 9. merry can
5. 1. bean/been 2. bare/bear 3. rains/reins 4. allowed/aloud 5. week/weak 6. stories/storeys 7. pane/pain
   8. read/red 9. bolder/boulder
6. 1. stretch 2. hugs 3. laps 4. stitch 5. spectacle 6. pardon 7. knit 8. Tear 9. leads
7. 1. stinking 2. shocking 3. warm 4. hair-raising 5. sticky 6. bare-faced 7. striking 8. rare 9. broken
8. 1D 2F 3I 4E 5H 6A 7G 8C 9B
9. 1F 2E 3D 4H 5B 6A 7I 8C 9G
10. 1G 2D 3I 4A 5H 6J 7B 8C 9F 10E
11. 1C 2G 3I 4H 5D 6A 7E 8F 9B
12. 1E 2G 3F 4I 5C 6H 7D 8A 9B
13. 1E 2G 3D 4H 5I 6A 7B 8C 9F
14. 1F 2G 3D 4I 5B 6A 7E 8J 9H 10C
15. 1G 2D 3H 4F 5J 6I 7B 8A 9E 10C
16. 1E 2I 3H 4G 5C 6B 7F 8D 9A
17. 1H 2I 3B 4D 5J 6F 7C 8A 9E 10G
18. 1. night 2. second hand 3. slip 4. beat/whip/batter 5. bright 6. scales 7. count 8. horns 9. single
    10. sleeping pills
19. 1D 2G 3E 4H 5I 6F 7A 8C 9B 10J
20. 1H 2F 3B 4D 5A 6C 7E 8G
21. 1E 2F 3I 4C 5H 6A 7G 8B 9D
22. 1. adult 2. acquaintance 3. net 4. archaeologist 5. antique 6. advice 7. alarm clock 8. diplomat 9. Poverty
23. 1. a towel 2. a river 3. a book 4. a comb 5. your word 6. a bottle 7. a tap 8. a stamp 9. a blackboard
24. 1G 2D 3A 4H 5B 6E 7I 8F 9C
25. 1F 2G 3I 4E 5H 6A 7D 8C 9B
26. 1C 2I 3A 4F 5H 6G 7B 8D 9E
27. 1G 2H 3A 4F 5B 6I 7D 8C 9E
28. 1E 2H 3F 4A 5I 6B 7J 8C 9G 10D
29. 1F 2G 3D 4A 5H 6E 7B 8J 9I 10C

Section 2

Lessons 33 to 38 are self-explanatory.
30. This road sign normally has ELDERLY PEOPLE written on it and appears near an Old People's Home.
31. Toblerone is, of course, the name of a kind of chocolate in a triangular shaped box.
32. The machine on the right has a guillotine on it.

Section 3

The misprint is printed first, followed by the correct word:
39. 1. mule-male 2. wife-life 3.bad-bar 4. licked-kicked 5. loving-room-living-room 6. plant-plane
    7. sell-tell 8. dead-deaf 9. chips-ships 10. cat-car
40. 1. pants-paints 2. lose-close 3. sing-sting 4. bear-beard 5. hopping-shopping 6. eats-beats 7. cars-cards
    8. pay-play 9. lock-clock 10. tea-team
41. 1. waiter-water 2. glove-love 3. pray-pay 4. hair-air 5. seat-sea 6. toilet-to let 7. soil-oil 8. army-arm
    9. monkey-money 10. gold-god
42. 1. blind-blond 2. wines-winds 3. smell-swell 4. harm-farm 5. decent-recent 6. hole-home 7. toads-loads
    8. fright-flight 9. shave-share 10. naked-named
43. 1. tail-trail 2. heat-heart 3. food-flood 4. tables-tablets 5. grow-growl 6. violet-violent 7. other-mother
    8. peasant-pleasant 9. pans-plans 10. lunch-launch
44. 1. horse-hose 2. wage-age 3. window-widow 4. threat-treat 5. stranglers-strangers 6. ghost-host 7. scar-car
    8. sport-spot 9. live-lie 10. pretty-petty
45. 1. bed-bid 2. frowned-drowned 3. will-well 4. ballet-ballot 5. deceived-received 6. menu-mend
    7. crows-crowd 8. calm-call 9. expensive-extensive 10. souffle-scuffle
46. 1. dies-dines 2. resents-presents 3. bride-bridge 4. disable-disabled 5. pets-pests 6. ant-anti 7. diving-driving
    8. rusty-trusty 9. hanged-changed 10. curse-course
47. 1. rabbits-rabbis 2. beast-best 3. strained-trained 4. cleaner-leaner 5. slimy-slim 6. friction-fiction
    7. cartoon-carton 8. members-embers 9. meditation-mediation 10. bright-right

Section 4

48. I don't know. It wasn't there this morning.
49. I'm not her father. I'm her mother.
50. And don't wear my clothes again.
51. I'm Martin. The baby's name is Paul.
52. That's not my dog.
53. My goodness! What happened to all the pencils, Miss?
54. I have taken your TV, your video and your jewellery. Now you know who sent you the ticket.
55. It's lonely here, now. Will you bring back the German and will you bring back the Frenchman, please.
56. If I fall out of the tree, shoot the dog.
57. You don't have to get angry because you don't know the answer.
58. Thirty-five years old.
59. Because I'm freezing cold.
60. I'll get you a spoon. My house doesn't have any electricity.
61. Then, who is looking after the shop?
62. I'm sorry, sir. You can't come into the hotel if you are not wearing a tie.
63. The man was your doctor.
64. Son, always remember that the first rule in business is – NEVER TRUST ANYBODY.
65. Likee speechee?
66. Now there is.
67. Looking at you, anybody would think that you had caused it.
68. That shows you how good my dust is.
69. Friends.
70. Sir Reginald, if you were my husband, I would drink it!
71. You have to be old and very rich to do that.
72. Me!
73. I don't know what you're complaining about. We have to walk back.
74. That's one.
75. Do you think the British are stupid! We'll go at night.
76. Go back. It's a trap. There's a second Spartan hiding behind the hill.
77. John, take the dog by the narrative and extinguish it.
78. Do you or do you not tell your partner?
79. You put your left leg in. You put your left leg out and you shake it all about. You do the Hokey Cokey and you turn around. That's what it's all about!
80. The pianist was my wife.
81. Let me have another look at that leg.
82. Missed.
83. And I say to the colonel, I'm Kirlov. Petrov lives upstairs. Now that, gentlemen, is true happiness.
84. He's not much of a truck driver either. He's just reversed over thirty motorcycles.
85. The dead vulture.
86. I see that we're back to one sandwich again.
87. I don't know who the person in white is, but that's Wee Davy next to him.
88. Congratulations. Many happy returns.
89. On the path to the next village you will see many bulls grazing. We must be careful not to step in any patunga as we walk along this path.
90. Good. By God! We're going to Glasgow!
91. Tonight's the night!
92. If you drink whisky, you won't be troubled by worms!